It's all Good

Deciphering <u>A Course In Miracles</u>
into Denials and Affirmations

Anonymous

Table of Contents

Chapter 1 : "I"	1
Chapter 2 : "We"	15
Chapter 3 : This realm of time, space and matter	74
Chapter 4 : Miracles and Actions for Good	87
Appendix 1 : Meditation – Inner Sensitivity – Teaching of Inner Christ	92
Appendix 2 : Meditation – Self Realization Fellowship – Paramahansa Yogananda	97
Appendix 3 : Prayer – Science of Mind – Ernest Holmes	102
Appendix 4 : Spiritual Treatment	107
Appendix 5 : Spiritual Treatment Meditation	111

Chapter 1 : "I"

With Emma Curtis Hopkins' instructions and techniques for denials and affirmations, I rephrased some of the text of <u>A Course of Miracles</u> to read as follows:

First Person, Singular

I am the Good in which I am seeking. I have not only been created fully, I have been created perfect. There is nothing I need to change. There is no emptiness in me. Because Good is perfect, I am perfect as well. I cannot lose this quality because it is inherent in what I am, a creation of Good.

I do not believe that what Good created can be changed by my own conscious mind. I do not believe that I can render what is perfect to something imperfect or lacking. I do not believe that I can distort the creations of Good, including myself. I do not believe that I can create or change myself or that alone, without connection to my Good, I can manage well.

True denial is a powerful protective device. Denial of error is a strong defense for Truth. I deny any belief that error can hurt me. In the service for Good, the denial of error frees my mind and re-establishes the freedom of my will. When my will is really free it cannot be misused, because it recognizes only Truth. I defend Truth instead of error.

I correct seeming error by stepping into the present and free myself from the past. I learn and practice improving my perception of Good. As my mind's focus becomes better and better, I get closer and closer to the perfection of Good until I no longer see duality. As I cross the bridge to my Good, I will no longer need this realm of time, space and matter to learn or practice. My Good provides me the total commitment required to accomplish this task.

I continue to believe only in what is Good. With my Good, I cannot experience bad therefore I have no need to escape bad. All lies literally disappear in the twinkling of an eye as they are merely a misperception. With Good, I am free from any bondage of this physical world.

Only Good has any value worthwhile. I keep my mind and my heart in my Good, which is my treasure. My Good removes all fear, doubt and ego from all my actions for Good. I do not acknowledge fear or evil. I do not give fear or evil my power. My power comes from and remains in my Good.

With Good, I am secure. I assume my natural talents provided by my Good. I refuse to believe in emptiness or that any lack exists in me because I am always connected with my Good. My Good keeps me spiritually awake.

Connected with Good, I am perfectly unaffected by all expressions of lack of love. I remain unshaken by seeming lack of love from without. The Good in and through me corrects the conditions proceeding from seeming lack of love in myself or others.

I do not have the ability to usurp the peace of Good. I do not seek peace or happiness externally from this physical world. Peace is an attribute of Good that I cannot find anywhere else but within my Good.

I cannot destroy Peace. Error cannot disrupt Peace. Peace cannot be used destructively. Peace is not beyond our understanding just as long as we are connected with our Good. I do not refuse Peace as I do not refuse my Good.

My Good is my offense and defense. My Good is my security and my protection. As inner Light is released within me, I no longer need to protect myself. My Good has created me invulnerable to deceit.

My spiritual eye sees only real beauty and cannot see error. The importance given to my physical senses wanes as my spirituality increases. There is no error in the spiritual realm. I do not associate with lack or loss. I correct distortion by letting my Good restore me.

My mind is in the service of my Good. I depend only upon my Good. In sharing my Good, I experience joy. My Good undoes any appearance of separation from Good and has already restored my mind to wholeness.

I perfectly trust my Good in all things. All other attempts to make myself comfortable are inappropriate. I do not entertain discomfort or pain. My Good makes this process effortless.

My Good actions are a result of my Good thinking. I emphasize my Good in all things. I have been healed and restored to sanity. I cannot be confused or sick. I do not own or recognize aspects of fear or evil.

My Good consciousness only has the ability to create Good. I only live in and learn from Good. I believe in Good mind over matter.

Healing is provided from the Spiritual realm. There are no physical means to healing that are lasting. Our bodies, senses and mind are only probes or drones used to learn, live and expand our Good. My true nature is neither matter or of this realm of matter, space and time

When a physical body is placed into near death, suspended animation, human hibernation, emergency preservation, deep hypothermic cardio arrest, etc., the mind does not become unconscious. Evidence and testimony reveal that mind continues without a body. The mind then seeks its Good, which is the same as when the mind is connected with the live body in this physical realm.

Good seeks the mind as well. The unconscious does not exist in the realm of Good because there is no unconscious mind. Good is eternal, infinite, all, and omnipresent, therefore Good cannot be unconscious. My mind is never separated from my Good. Good always encompasses Itself.

My Superconscious mind is filled with Good. Through my will and desire in this physical realm, my conscious mind can go to the subconscious mind in meditation to then ask the Superconscious mind in prayer for my Good. My Good from the Superconscious fills my subconscious mind and creates my Good in the physical. In the physical, I only focus on my Good and deny all other misperception.

Physicians and Physicists, as a stereotype, only study and learn about the physical and within their practice they are ignorant of the Spiritual or Spiritual methodology. Therefore, they frequently deny their Good, but accept their negative misperceptions as Truth.

My Good is not frightening or harmful. I am not afraid to allow my Good to heal me or you. I no longer require physical remedies or material agents for wrongly perceived bodily, mental or emotional illness. With my Good, I cannot entertain fear. My level of communication with my Good has been raised.

My Good is perfect and requires no correction. My Good has provided me only correct thinking. My Good has corrected my mind; I have no misperceptions in my mind. Misperceptions are no longer formed in my mind. I am perfect, whole and complete. My Good is always ready to restore Good whenever it is perceived as being missing.

My consciousness has been healed and I live in my right mind. I recognize that mind is the only creative level, and that its errors are healed by Good. I deny any destructive potential of my mind.

Good has reinstated pure constructive powers in my mind to be used for Good. Levels of confusions are undone.

I am no longer endowed with self-initiation or self-reliance. My Good illuminates me as electricity illuminates the light bulb. As my mind looks toward the light of Good, my body is brought into alignment.

My Good is awake in me. There is no defilement of my mind. I have turned away from trusting my physical senses or of evaluating this physical world. The senses I have received from my Good, sense only Good and detect nothing else. Channeling Good results in the awareness of omnipresent Good.

All discomfort is removed with my awareness of all powerful Good. All aspects of time, space and matter are temporary. Good can easily manipulate time, space or matter. I no longer perform in this limited physical world. I am not dependent upon time, space or matter. The need for lower order concerns has been abolished. I coexist with my Good in timelessness. \

The perfection of Good lies within me. Good encompasses me in love, power, knowledge, wisdom, understanding, etc. I deny error and affirm the Truth. My faith in Good removes all worry of what I should say or do. Where ever I am, I am content because my Good is with me. My Good has made me truly helpful. My constructive acts for Good are not of my will or volition because my Good directs me.

There is never a reason for me to be afraid of my thinking. With the grace of my Good, I cannot do something loveless. The perfect Love of my Good is the only remedy for lack of Love. I always remain fully aware of the real power of Good. This remedy removes fear.

Good never sleeps. Erroneous conclusions have been dispelled from my mind through my constant connection with my Good. I have given up all my unnecessary defenses against my Good. In Good, I cannot be bitter, afraid or suffer. In Good, I cannot be bad. Good adequately protects the Truth that I cannot be condemned, punished or persecuted. In Good, I am free of any belief in scarcity or poverty.

I do not taint my Good with any form of distortion. I do not accuse myself or anyone else of an evil past. I have no need for retribution or vengeance. I cannot be rejected or abandoned by my Good. My Good channels mercy, love and kindness through me.

In my Good, I cannot be weak, vulnerable or destructive. I cannot be accused of any wrong doing. With my Good, I cannot be scolded or terrorized. My Good provides me strength alongside my innocence. I am blessed and pure of heart.

Knowing my Good is my strength. I associate my strength with my innocence. My innocent mind has provided me all things Good. My Good keeps me whole. My innocent mind cannot project evil attributes unto others. My Good mind can only honor others.
As I believe in my Good, I am free to live only in Good. I cannot shroud innocence or grace in darkness. Perfect innocence is wisdom. Perfect innocence is strength. I cannot blind myself from my Good. My Good radiates Good in all things. Good can withstand any assault. Nothing can destroy Good. .

I have received the gift of atonement. There is nothing I need sacrifice. I understand the power of innocence. I am radiant. I cannot conceive any opposition to Good. In the realm of Good I cannot see or apply duality. I conceive only Good. There is only Truth. Lies or distortions do not exist. I maintain a firm commitment to my Good. I cannot deny my Goodness. My innocence is total.

I apply my Good universally. I never misperceive and I always see truly. I only see that which exists which is my Good. I do not lack confidence in myself or in others. Knowing that nothing but Good exists, I can see only perfection in all things.

I use my mind in accordance with the will of Good. I cannot be held back, imprisoned or possessed by anything that does not exist. In Good, my will is free. I am of one mind with Good. I experience Heaven now and forever. Nothing can prevail against Good.

Good has awakened my mind. I experience true innocence. My heart has been rendered pure. I neither attack nor defend. True perception requires neither. I have withdrawn any incorrect faith in distortions and lies. I have cancelled all misperception in the way I see others. I have accepted their Good.

Good established perfect peace and integration with one another. I recognize myself and all others to be perfectly Good. There is no illness and all misperception of illness has already been healed. I cannot sense separation from my Good.

There is strength in knowledge of Good. My knowledge and true perceptions of Good foster more Good. My Good produces strong affirmation of Good. Knowledge of Good is timeless. Because of knowledge, questioning or answering are unnecessary in the realm of Good.

I neither see myself nor my mind existing in time, space or matter. I am eternal. My physical body is unrequired. My perception, vision and spiritual sight have been replaced with knowledge. I know and see only facts of Good.

Only my knowledge of Good can create in its image. I know my Good. Good has opened my true eyes and true thought. I am certain that I know Good as myself. My certainty does not require action.

Good communicates certainty and knowledge which has replaced both perception and time. Good is stable. I know Good and accept its certainty. I cannot see error in others nor do I see anyone as a stranger or foe. One mindedness with my Good is without confusion. Good wills my mind to know Good.

The egocentric mind is divided and confused and cannot recognize or produce Good. All misperception comes from an egocentric mind. The egocentric mind or will cannot exist in my Good. I did not create myself. I see myself as Good created me, therefore I cannot see nor attack error. Good provides me real strength. Good has no degrees or intervals, therefore I cannot perceive conflict or perceive without love.

Good permeates all. This experience of time, space and matter is not the world of misperception. I cannot perceive inaccurately. As I remain in my Good, perception is not required. Good cannot be limited in power. My conscious mind chooses to ignore and deny any realm of misperception. I always remain in my Good.

Good is not the threat, because it has never considered anything in opposition to Good. Good knows that miscreation or misperception cannot exist. I remember only my Good. There is no need to counteract error because my will is united with my Good. My choices are sane. I listen only to my Good. I know only peace.

I experience the real strength of Good because my Good flows through me. I possess superconscious abilities. With the knowledge from my Good I am sure in every thought or action. My will can only be aligned with my Good. I lack nothing nor do I have any reason to compensate for lack. My Good does not need to be invented or improved.

The Kingdom of Good is not of this physical world. Time, space or matter will not satisfy me nor can it deceive me. I cannot manipulate time, space or matter to satisfy myself or anyone else.

With Good, I cannot exist in any mixture of time, space or matter. I do not cling to or use any methodology of duality in a realm of space, time and matter.

My Good is stable and consistent. I cannot regard myself as separate from my Good. I am perfectly stable and consistent as my Good permeates me. My knowledge of Good is also stable and consistent.

Wisdom is the use of pure knowledge of Good. I maintain the knowledge that I am completely connected with my Good. My knowing my Good does not require that I do anything in this world of misperception except to perceive Good. I fully cooperate with my Good. I accept the purity of knowledge from my Good.

With the knowledge provided from my Good, there is no reason for me to be ingenious. Being self-ingenious does not serve my Good. Compromise creates only confusion and difficulty. I need not evaluate, discriminate or judge.

Knowing that I am my Good, my knowledge is complete. My Good is inseparable. My Good is beyond perception. My Good is beyond any doubt. There are no degrees in the equilibrium of eternal and infinite Good.

I do not accuse myself or anyone else of any wrong doing or wrong thinking. I know only Good. There are no separate, incorrect minds. Infinite, eternal and homogeneous is my mind.

I am not a mixture. I do not perceive. I do not judge. I did not lose peace. I do not reject or abandon my Good. I only emphasize Good whether it be in me or you. There is nothing that can be found wanting. Such concepts cannot be formed or exist in my mind. I do not believe in the unreal.

Reality is not mine to select from. My Good is the experience of deep peace. Error in myself or anyone else cannot exist. I do not need judgement in any form. I do not need to organize. My knowledge replaces perception and judgement.

Nothing can be used against me. I can never experience danger. I have no weapons. I cannot be tired. I cannot weary or worry. I do not mock. No one can be unworthy.

I am not the author of reality, therefore I do not have any authority. But, I cannot doubt my existence. My creation was not anonymous. I am certain that Good authored me and I cannot usurp Good because I am not the author of Good.

I only cherish Good. I have accepted all that is Good. I hold on to my Good. My Good offers mercy. Good is incapable of injustice. My thoughts, words and actions only reflect Good. I look upon Good without judgement.

My position in Good is unassailable and impregnable. My mind is not split. I cannot comprehend contradiction or confusion. I cannot conceive or project delusions. I am not in competition. I cannot be frightened or punished. I am never unhappy. I give up desire. Rejection or abandonment are impossible. I have not lost my Good. I merely know that Good is everywhere and cannot be lost.

I have accepted my inheritance. I cannot deny my Good. There are no bonds upon the will of Good. I did not create myself nor do I not have the power to destroy my Good given purpose. Good is my peace.

I cannot be in opposition to my Good nor did I give myself power to be in opposition to my Good. There are no barriers to my Good. There is no limitation or rationing of my Good. I cannot be in segments.

The will of Good is sufficient. I will only my Good. I know I am Good. I only know and accept my Good. My mind is strong and has the power of Good. My Good is a foundation that cannot be shaken. My mind is in service to my Good. There is no conflict in Good. There is no death in Good.

I am forever unwilling to depart from my foundation in Good. From my devotion to my Good, I am inspired. The spirit of Good is within me. I am enlightened and there can be no seeming darkness, fatigue or dejection.

With my Good, I cannot be egocentric. The spirit of Good speaks through me. My life in Good cannot experience lack of power, reparation or death. In Good, there is no waste.

My Good cannot be challenging. Easy, effortless and rewarding success is the only path my Good can lead me on. I have complete trust in my Good. With my Good in, around and through me, I have complete trust in myself and others I encounter. I am consistent in my trust of my Good.

My Good never fails. No one thought opposes another. There can be no contradiction in Good. Conflict is impossible. There can be no wish to deceive or create conflict. I experience only perfect harmony, peace and honesty.

As I trust my Good, I can only be honest. Nothing I say or do can contradict my Good. I do not have any thoughts in opposition to my Good. As I am in total agreement with my Good, my words and actions only relay Good to others. The peace of mind that comes from my Good makes it impossible for me to deceive or be in conflict with myself or anyone else. As I allow the will of my Good to manage all things in my experience, nothing can challenge my success.

To not seek my Good would be insane; harm and guilt are products of insanity. Without my Good, I do not have the ability to judge correctly. Without my Good, I will only deceive myself. But

I am never without my Good. As I focus only on Good, harm is impossible and guilt cannot exist.

Because my Good provides me trust and honesty, everything I encounter is acceptable and delightful. My Good is wholly gentle, joyous and peaceful.

Since my Good is unlimited source, I need not fear giving up or losing anything. I am not frightened of generously giving my Good to others because my Good endlessly flows through me. Generosity and helpfulness are not a dreadful burden or unpleasant task because Good is not unpleasant, dreadful or arduous.

I never have to wait anxiously for my Good nor can I ever be frustrated with the results from my Good. Time has no meaning in my realm provided by my Good. Everything from my Good serves to benefit my experience, thinking, memory and reality whether I am looking into the future, past or present. With my Good there are no mistakes or error in the past, present or future.

Since I am completely protected by my Good, I have no reason to defend or attack myself. I have no thoughts that need defense against my Good. My safety comes from not maintaining defensive or offensive positions or systems. My Good does not allow any danger to exist. As I experience only Good, my trust in Good increases.

Knowledge and consistent experience of Good is my faith and trust. My consistent faith and trust in Good create more of the same. I do not tire or fatigue from the experience of Good. My thought or emotions in Good cannot be diverted or deceived. I do not condemn anyone or anything as being evil. Forgiveness is unnecessary in the realm of Good because there is nothing to forgive. I give forth only Good.

When I speak, I clarify and strengthen Good. I see and hear only Good in others. I am equal to and alike all others from Good. My strength lies in the gentleness of Good and as a result I inevitably experience joy. Suffering, pain or evil cannot come from or exist in Good. I am certain that I am loved and cared for by only Good. There can be no attack or grief in Good. Only the voice for Good can successfully direct me.

I have no reason to fear change because my Good is consistent. I believe that everyone has Good to give out to all they encounter. Everyone I encounter contributes to my Good.

Nothing contradicts my Good. My motives cannot be opposed to Good. I have relinquished all ties with the physical and material for neither have a mind or can know what Good is. The material and the physical do not have the ability to communicate with Good, however Good can use the physical and material for purposes of Good.

With the knowledge of Good, I have nothing to learn. Knowing of my Good, I cannot respond to anything with fear. I cannot envision a world separated from my Good. I am not the creator of my thought system, but my Good assists with the responsibility to guard against and remove all thoughts that do not induce Good.

My Good is always gentle and leads me gently back to my Good. I can only follow and abide in the laws for Good because of the nature in which Good created me. My Good is always in accordance and cannot clash with anything. I do not see ego nor do I communicate with it because there is no such thing as ego in the realm of Good.

As a teacher of Good, my goal is to not teach Good but instead give forth Good. The Good people I encounter have no need for a teacher. My worth is not established by teaching or learning.
There is nothing that I can think, do, make or desire that can establish or reestablish my worth. There is nothing for me to

dispute. Ego cannot effect my thoughts or actions. My spirit is established only in Good and there can be no contradiction, delusion or confusion with the law of Good. I am utterly devoted to my Good.

I have no need for praise of myself. I do not have to overcome doubt. I do not need to whistle in the dark to overcome fear. Insecurity, doubt, fear, death nor dark do not exist in Good. With my Good, my mind knows what is real and what is not real. I have accepted the one and only true reality of Good. There is nothing for me to learn or change. I am still and know Good as real.

Neither my Good nor I are the author of fear. I cannot create anything unlike my Good. I am in this existence only to fulfill my function for Good. I only believe the credible and perform likewise in accordance with Good. I cannot avoid Good and Good cannot leave me. I am continuously and eternally connected with my Good.

Perception of the physical and material as anything other than Good can only be a delusion which cannot serve Good. My experience of the joy of Good leaves no room for any delusional emotions. I do not invest in the material or physical. I have left any and all belief in the physical or material behind. I only invest in the realm of Good. I am no longer attached to myself, therefore I am no longer I.

***

Now, how did that feel? I put down enough material, so that the reader could get past the initial resistance and experience the realm of denial and affirmation. Pretty amazing stuff? With continual immersion, this is how the conscious mind is healed. With the raising of one's consciousness, the physical will correspond.

Chapter 2 : "We"

So my first snag was that "I" is still "EGO" and to be joined as one, perhaps reading and writing these affirmations in First Person Plural would be more appropriate. So I continue with my exercises of re-writing ACIM into "denials and affirmations":

1st Person, Plural

With Good, we effectively reject any unconscious distortions or any power that could block the consciousness of our Good. As creations from Good, We cannot and do not hold misperceptions rigidly in place. We never experience a lack of Love, therefore we can never express hostility, vengeance, self-debasement or triumph. It is profound error to imagine that fantasies of evil could be true. This would be the incorrect use of the imagination. Evil is impossible to perceive as long as we remain connected with our Good. We use our conscious mind and imagination to remain always within Good.

With the higher power of Good, we do not confuse impulses for Good with physical impulses. We will never find happiness using the instruments of this physical world. We do not use our Good given physical impulses inappropriately to create guilt or depression. Our associations with the physical and material will never provide us lasting pleasure. Real pleasure comes from true Good. We immediately correct any error in our perception with the knowledge that the use of anything physical or external cannot create our prosperity, peace or bring us to true happiness and joy.

Our beautiful souls were created from Good to create Good. The physical eye only sees the physical. While in this body in this physical realm, we enlarge our vision of Good so that we develop real and true vision through the spiritual eye. Learning and practicing the enlargement of our consciousness toward Good will decrease the importance of the body and this physical realm, making our transformation to Good safe, calm, easy and effortless.

Fantasy and projection can never control our external environment satisfactorily. It is a misperception to think that the external environment can satisfy our internal needs. Only Good can satisfy all our needs and Good is of the spiritual realm and not the physical realm. Through our experience of the physical realm and the wisdom that we have gained, we now devote ourselves to our restoration to greater Good. Our conscious mind, alone, cannot distinguish the Truth from the false. We need the force of Good to assist us.

We have developed a strong desire to connect our conscious and subconscious mind with Good. We have arrived at the point where we know that we can no longer serve two masters. We have developed a strong conviction that fantasies, distortions and delusions become totally unnecessary and cannot satisfy the nature of true reality.

Our conscious mind cannot change one iota of Good. The misperception of this world as chaotic, sad or horrific is based upon lies that can never be true. We cannot render Good into something imperfect or unintelligent. We cannot make Good unloving and reckless. We cannot manage our lives or this world successfully without the assistance of Good.

We have stopped calling a lie, the Truth and calling the Truth, a lie. The physical and material will not bring us permanent happiness. Striving for more material and sensual gain to satisfy our conscious mind is like making a deal with the Devil: for thirty minutes of pleasure, the Devil will provide you thirty years of pain. However, there is no Devil, nor can we make deals with something that does not exist.

Good has created the soul as perfect and whole. Our soul is unaffected by any expression of seeming lack. We do not have the power to usurp our Good; such an idea is only a lie. Our souls will never be harmed by our physical experiences. Pain and suffering can only be imagined.

With Good, we cannot be afraid of anything. Without our Good, we believe in only the conscious mind and the physical world our senses and mind can perceive. Thus we seem to become limited and frightened. Our conscious mind fears pain, loss, discomfort, death, rejection and so on. To be free of discomfort we deny any limitation, pain and fear. We correct our perception by uniting our conscious mind with our Good. We use our spiritual eye that Good provides us and not trust our own thinking and the data from of our limited sense organs.

The human mind along with the collective consciousness of all existing human minds is limited and only a small fragment of the intelligence, knowledge, wisdom and understanding of the Superconscious. As souls united with our Good, we cannot be shaken or deceived by the human or race mind. We stand fast in the greater power and intelligence of our Good.

It is not a bitter pill for the physical mind to serve our Good. Contrarily, it is the only Truth that will deliver us satisfaction. We do not underestimate the necessity for staying connected with our Good in our life at all times. We are not independent conscious minds; we are connect to the Good of the Superconscious. We free our conscious minds by denying all error and affirming the Truth. We instantly change any perceived threat back to the nothing from which it came. We are steadfast and certain. We do not waver.

Only Good exists. Good projects peace through us in our time, space, matter realm. Good helps us withdraw from the confusion and meaningless lies of this perceived world. Disassociation and flight from error are perfectly appropriate. It is much easier to defend Truth than it is to defend this physical realm. Our Good makes all of our effort and collective measures sufficient. We are consistent with how much we treasure our Good. Our Good picks up the bill when we are short.

We no longer defend ourselves to maintain our separation from our Good. Good undoes the separation and restores wholeness to our mind. Our Good makes us invulnerable to fear. Thoughts and emotions of fear and separation are now undone. Our Good defends us as long as we consciously remain with our Good.

We do not delay or procrastinate in our Actions for Good. We look past error toward Truth. We trust our Good. As children of Good, we are entitled to perfect comfort. We lose our egocentricity as we commune with our Good. We perceive only Good in our mind, our body and the world as means of healing all perceived separation from our Good.

Our alignment with Good removes fear. Healing is the result and we are no longer ill. We are cured. Fear and insanity are removed at all levels. All symptoms of any illness are gone because we no longer believe that our body can create error. United with our Good, the mind cannot create illness inside the body and the body cannot create illness in the mind.

We can control being afraid by focusing on our Good. We no longer raise lies to levels of importance. We now correct insane thought and behavior. We cannot foster confusion. We have become responsible for what we think. Our behavior no longer has autonomy as we place what we think under the guidance from our Good. We do not tolerate insane thinking.

What we do comes from what we think. While remaining in our Good, we are never afraid. As we place what we think under the guidance from Good, we cannot separate ourselves from the Truth by "giving" autonomy to our thinking, emotions or our behavior. Our responsibility is to keep our conscious mind focused on Good. Then our thinking, emotions and behavior conform with Good. We no longer are willing to keep our conscious mind separate from our Good. We do not tolerate a wandering mind and before we act we always confirm that our conscious thoughts are aligned with our Good.

We no longer attempt to heal at the symptom level. Correction occurs with the focus of our conscious mind toward our Good. We are always aware that this is our responsibility and we always ask our Good for help in this matter. We no longer separate ourselves from our Good. We immediately recognize that fear, worry, suffering, pain, conflict, confusion, depression, anxiety, etc. are signs that we are no longer connected with our Good. To instantly correct these symptoms, we ask to have our conscious mind reconnected with our Good and for the strength to keep our mind from wandering.

By keeping our conscious mind focused in Good we cannot experience conflict with what we think, do or feel. With our experiences of Good and being separated from our Good in this physical world, we develop a strong will to remain with our Good. There is no strain in keeping our conscious mind aligned with our Good.

With Good, we cannot express fear. With Good, we express love beyond our comprehension. With Good, we come to know what true value and real worth is. Then we express respect from the worthy to the worthy. We no longer have any reason for a remedy, healing or cure.

We appreciate the true power of mind. What we think, creates. Our thought and belief in Good combine into a power surge that can literally move mountains. All thinking produces form at some level, so we respect only Good thinking

To remain in Truth, there are no "idle" thoughts. All destructive thinking is dangerous. In Good, fear does not exist. We do not complain or entertain fear. We carefully guard our thoughts throughout the day. We accept the power and miracles from Good to accomplish this. We vehemently avoid miscreation with the incorrect use of thought.

We have become used to miracles and miraculous thinking. We maintain full realization of our power with thought. We constantly choose to receive miracles from our Good which keeps our minds straight. We are not afraid of our Good and as we receive our Good, we are no longer afraid of ourselves or of others. We choose the miracle of Good and reject all else.

We are no longer egocentric. We no longer believe that we can manufacture our Good. We know that we receive our Good through our meditation and prayers. We know what to ask for because we know what Good is and what is not Good. Because we have received Good, we have also developed readiness, confidence and mastery.

We consciously maintain our focus on our Good. We have become invulnerable to misperception. Cause and effect now mean that our Good creates our Good. This is the difference between creation and miscreation.

We immediately correct erroneous idle thoughts. All negative perceptions are ephemeral, unsatisfactory and faulty. In Good, judgement is unnecessary. Because the false has been sorted from our minds, we experience true freedom in our Good.

We are masters of love. In love, fear cannot exist, therefore fear has no power. There no longer is any conflict between love and fear within ourselves. Compromise between sometimes love and sometimes fear has been released.

Good is eternal and infinite. Good is magnificence and splendor. We are always in awe of our Good. Our Good is the doorway to true life, beauty and love. In Good, there is no scarcity of love, mercy and forgiveness. Good adequately protects the Truth.

Good induces correct perception of our reality. Our Good demonstrates unconditional forgiveness, mercy and love. Readiness for our Good becomes easy and effortless. We need not sacrifice. Persecution, condemnation, blame or punishment are impossible in our Good.

In Good, there is no room for bad. Good does not entertain distortion of the Truth. Assumptions are impossible. Our Good cannot reject us. Our Good cannot be twisted. We do not attempt to shroud light in darkness. Our Good radiates Truth and sheds only blessings. We arose from perfect innocence. We are perfectly aware of all things true and give no recognition to nonexistent evil. Nothing can destroy our Good. We believe firmly that we are released from all error.

We have learned our lessons well. All sense of separation has disappeared and all confusion has vanished. We are one mind and one will aligned with our Good. We are perfectly integrated in peace. We, the innocent have had our hearts purified. We defend true perception. We know not how to attack anything or anyone.

Our single purpose creates perfect integration and establishes the peace of God. We who are innocent understand fully this peace. Our Good has created us as merciful. We neither fear nor sacrifice. Our strength and our innocence are not in conflict. Our strength is our pure mind that follows only Truth. Our innocent mind has everything Good.

Honor is the natural greeting of the truly loved to others. We are truly radiant. We do not see darkness. We only see the light that dispels all darkness. We stand firm and do not compromise. In the realm of Good, polarities cannot exist.

The innocence of Good, without guilt, shame or remorse, is our true state of mind. Our innocence is not a partial attribute. Our wisdom is that we apply our innocence universally.

It is impossible for us to deny our Good. Our solace is infinite and eternal. We are adamant about always perceiving our Good in all things we experience. Our Good is the only thing that exists.

We do not lack confidence in anyone we know or encounter. We perceive everything as it is, Good. Only what Good creates has any real existence, therefore what is not Good cannot exist. There is nothing to heal, for sickness, disease, illness or death do not exist.

We cannot validate the invalid. We do not suffer distortions of separation from our Good. We invest our adamant faith only in what is true. Because we see all as Good, we validate everyone's Good.

We do not confuse knowledge with perception. We know our Good for certain. The knowledge of Good is all powerful. In our knowledge of Good, there is nothing that can disturb or disrupt our Good. The certainty of our Good provides us strength and invulnerability. The basis for knowledge is true perception. Knowledge is the adamant confirmation of Good as the only Truth.

We know the one and only Truth. Our knowledge is timeless and unquestionable. With our knowledge of Good, we no longer need questions or answers because we are always certain. We do not need to ask questions when we already know the answers. Our Good affirms that we know the Truth.

We are not subject to transitory states. Our sight can only be true. In the realm of Good, we no longer require physical senses or locomotion. We have ceased to ask questions. We no longer need a future or a past. We are stable in our unchanged state of Good.

We recognize our Good in all things. To know yourself is to be certain in your knowledge of Good. To know someone is to know Good. We recognize our Good in our neighbors and we honor them. We recognize others as our Good. No one is our stranger. We know and honor everyone. We always recognize Good in all things and people.

We recognize with true love. Our Good is not a stranger. Our Good is always welcome in our household. The certainty of our Good brings security and peace. Our Good provides us love and we, in turn, love our Good. Our Good communicates with us constantly. We only know of Good.

Our Good has no degrees or quantities. There is no need to measure or categorize Good. We have no need to separate or divide ourselves or our reality. Consciousness of space, time or matter is unnecessary. Our consciousness of our Good is infinite and eternal.

We are superconscious. We cannot nor have we ever split our consciousness. We cannot be a drop in the ocean of consciousness, rather we are the whole. We are continuously connected to our Good. Our consciousness cannot be on separated or separate levels. Our consciousness can only exist in the domain of our Good.

Our Good provides us real strength and correct will. In our Good, we cannot deceive or be deceived. We have no need to question our Good because our Good provides us omniscience. In our Good, we are without confusion. We are in accord only with our Good.

We can never be strangers to one another. Attack of one another is as impossible as harboring fear. We do not need to exchange, translate or take from one another.

We will only the knowledge of Good. There is no ambiguity in Good. Our mind cannot be uncertain or confused. We neither produce nor need to escape confusion. We associate with the omniscience that comes from our Good. We know that no miscreation can exist. Good erases all miscreations and misperceptions brought under its guidance.

Good does not provide separate and limited levels of experience. Perception is meaningless and undesirable. We neither will separation nor perception. There is no separation to heal, therefore healing is unnecessary.

We did not create our mind. Our mind's purpose is to be in service to our Soul. Good has provided our souls with omnipotence. To separate our mind from our soul would only cause insanity. As we neither consider insane words, emotions or thoughts, we never consider insane actions or the condition of insanity. Our choice is sanity. Good knows us only in sanity and peace.

Our Good created our soul as eternal. Our resurrection is our return to knowledge. We want for nothing. We need not manufacture or invent. We are stable. We do not disagree. We know ourselves. We know who and what we are. We know our purpose. Our knowing is not open to interpretation.

The Superconscious is our Good. Our conscious mind is connected to the Superconscious Soul and communication is possible through meditation and correct prayer. This is how we remember correctly what we are. The surety of Good remains in our Soul. By uniting with our Good, we remember our Soul and its knowledge. The purpose of Soul is for Good.

Our knowledge does not require ingenuity. Our knowledge has released all lies and confusion. Our knowledge shows us how to pray. We know what to pray for. Good is our source and our real function.

Our Good does not contain duality. Evaluation of our Good is as unnecessary as organizing our Good. There is neither more Good or less Good, there is just Good. We do not serve multiple masters. We have everything and there is infinite bounty left over. We cannot conceive of any form of lack.

We select Good as the only sane choice available. We live in the one and only Good where the knowledge of ourselves is perfectly clear. We are completely aware of the perfect quality of our Good. Our knowledge of Good transcends knowledge of all physical laws. Our Soul knows our Good completely. We are in constant communion with our Good. We are inseparable from our Good. How beautiful indeed are our thoughts. Our knowledge is beyond doubt.

We know each other only as Good knows us. We have no need to condemn because we already know our Good. We never mock, ridicule or scorn. We cannot be degraded or disgraced. We cannot worry or become weary and disheartened. We never tire.

Our cognition only emphasizes the Good. We accept only Good. We have no reason to reject our Good. We have no belief in or time for the unreal. Reality of Good cannot be manipulated or altered. We cherish our Good and our Good cherishes us.

We are not the author of reality, therefore we desire no authority. There is no competition for authority over others. We have no use for weapons, defense or attack. We do not have power to usurp our Good or each other. We are not under any form of coercion. We can find nothing dangerous. We cannot be punished. We have accepted our inheritance from Good. We do not deny our Good nor do we have any problem with the authority of Good.

We are not the author of delusion. We are happy Souls. We know our creator. Rejection of our Good is impossible. We can neither usurp nor reject our Good. We cannot lose our Good. We always know where our Good is.

We are not the creators of our Good. Good created us whole and complete, therefore we do not envision ourselves as pieces or mixtures of Good. Our reality cannot be divided into segments of desire. Our recognition of Good requires no organizing. We are sufficient and have no need for desire or wishes. We know exactly that we are creations of perfect Good. As we will our Good our Good becomes evident.

We look upon our reality without judgment. We cannot be imprisoned by judgment because we have been created free. Prisons can only be made from matter to entrap us in time and space. Our mind and our soul are not made of matter nor do they exist in time and space. The prison of matter, space and time is made of nothing, based upon nothing and therefore cannot hold us. Nor can there be any evil force in competition and opposition to our Good that can hold us in the realm of time, space and matter.

Life in the world of time, space and matter can be of no real worth because peace is our natural heritage. The system that we are presently living in exists only in time, not in eternity. We are not trapped in this system but exist here voluntarily deriving our experience of Good from it. But Good does not exist in time but rather in eternity. As much as we search and try, Good cannot be found in space or matter. The worthless and meaningless trinkets of time and space cannot distract us from seeking our true Good.
A realm of nonexistence cannot be our prison. We choose to accept our Good and we always remain in the Kingdom of Good.

Our belief in Good creates our reality. We only have the power to create Good, not destroy It. That is our only purpose. Our reliance is upon our Good for power. Our Good gave us Its knowledge freely and we do not have the knowledge to misuse our power for destructive purposes. We did not receive power to create ourselves, therefore we can only use our power for Good purposes.

Knowledge cannot deceive us nor our perceptions. Our senses and our conscious mind cannot lie to us. We have discovered that the images we perceive in this realm of time, space and matter can only be Good. We are free of all thoughts of separation from our Good.

We do not have the power to make false images. Our minds cannot be split and exist in multiple realms. Our conscious mind cannot be split from our Superconscious mind. We are free of fear and delusion.

As we divide the atom into smaller and smaller parts, we discover there is no foundation to matter. As we look out further and further into what we call space, we see no limit. The borders to what we call the universe are infinity. As we change our focus from physics to metaphysics, the physical boundaries we have imagined dissolve into the nothingness of which they are made up.

The only foundation which cannot be dissolved is that of metaphysics. There is no beginning nor an end. There is no entropy or atrophy. Everything in our science of physics is built upon nothingness. However, in this imagined realm of time, space and matter, our conscious mind can never be in conflict and confused.

In the physical realm, we can only perceive with a correct conscious mind. Our science of time, space and matter has witnessed the existence of the superconscious, nonlocal mind which cannot be measured or observed by physical means. Only Good can witness Good. Testifying to Good keeps Good into our conscious mind.

Only this imaginary realm of time, space and matter can have a beginning or an end. This realm cannot produce Good, but we can experience our Good everywhere.

Duality is irreconcilable. There can be no death if there is life. There can be no dark if there is light. There can be no perception of this physical realm when there is total knowledge of our Good.

In our Good, our Souls are still at peace. Our oneness with our Good has no mental or emotional conflict. In Good, our thoughts are correct because all knowledge only exists in our Good. As a result of genuine devotion to Good, we are always filled with Good. With inspiration from Good, there can be no fatigue or temptation. We remain at peace knowing only our Good.

Our Soul is inspired. To be egocentric is to be dispirited, but we are never without Spirit. To be centered in Good is to be inspired. We are always enthused with the Spirit of our Good. We cannot disclaim our knowledge from Good because our Soul never departs from its foundation in Good.

We cannot nor do not suffer from symptoms of being human. We do not nor need not cling to this physical world of time, space and matter. We are revitalized in a realm of Good with no desire otherwise. We continually reenact our Good without boredom, dullness, tedium or glumness. Being all wise established by our Good, we cannot entertain any foolish thoughts, words or actions. We repeat the excitement of our Good endlessly.

We do not have the authority to reject our Good. We have an endless supply of Good. We do not have a variety of human symptoms. Our mind cannot be split between an ego versus our Soul. Our authority rests in the ability to demand abundant Good.

We are opposed to anything that is not in the realm of our Good. Any imagined separation from our Good can only be erroneous. Anything from ego is irreconcilable with our Good. Ego cannot communicate or demand anything from Good. Anything from the world of ego is incomplete and contradictory, therefore we profess only our Good. We share our Good with conviction. Our Soul only knows Good and cannot perceive anything else.

Ego is singular, self-sufficient, self-centered and individual. No such thing can exist in our Good. We are plural, inter-dependent, altruistic and united. Therefore a worthless ego has been rejected and abandoned into the nothingness from which it came.

Our Good leaves no room for ego, time, space, material or physical properties. Relinquishment of any and all concepts of the existence of an ego is not fearful or difficult. In fact we do not have to relinquish ego or the world that is based upon ego because as we focus on our Good. We never had the power to relinquish something that does not exist. The ego and this physical world have no power over our Soul, so there is nothing our Soul needs to renounce.

Focusing on our Good reveals that there is only one Truth. Our Good will always assist us in guarding our thoughts from diversion or distortion of the Truth. We can only believe and follow the one true law of Good.

We neither fear nor dispute our creation by our Good. By our Good, we are always protected from imaginary bogeymen.

Our worth is not established by our doing, learning or our teaching. Our worth has been established by our Good. We are Good and require no forgiveness.

We do not suffer from delusions which debate our Good and true reality. Our Soul is never at stake. Nothing can steal or pervert our Soul for it is always one with our Good. We are part of a reality of Good which stands unchanged and is out of reach from anything other than Good.

We fulfill the only function that we can which is to receive and appreciate our Good. We can never be impoverished. We live within the many mansions of our Good. Our Good is inevitable. Our Soul is always joyous. We make no investments in ego or its fearful consequences. We listen only to the joyous sound of our Good. We are not perishable nor is what we receive from our Good.

Our Soul needs no humility or salvation. Our Soul has recognized Its radiance and gladly sheds Its Good. We have inherited the

Kingdom of Good. The beauty, dignity and power of our Soul is beyond doubt, beyond perception and stands forever as the mark of love from our Good and we are worthy of such a gift. Our Soul is far beyond need for protection or control.

Our ego and this physical world hold no importance in the eternal Kingdom of Good. We cannot be tempted into hanging on to anything from time, space or matter. There is no need for tribulation.

Knowledge of our Good is complete and we need no perception of an individual self. The ego that our conscious mind perceives as a body and thought system cannot exist in our Good. History of the past or prophesy of the future are not required in the realm of Good. We cannot repeat errors because in Good, we cannot err.

In the reality of Good, perception of an ego cannot occur because the concept of an individual ego is not a thought based in Good. There is neither equilibrium nor equality on earth. The physical world of matter and ego require constant change and instability. Our Good is unalterable. Our knowledge of our Good only applies immaterial thought.

Besides, in the realm of time, space and matter, our actions and thoughts can never satisfy our ego or another's ego, for time, space, matter and moods are always changing. With the power of Good, we always correct our vision by denying the delusion of ego. We deny the illusion of time, space or matter by maintaining our focus on our Good.

Our Good would never allow us to corrupt our knowledge with belief systems. To believe in something is only a function of ego. Having to maintain a belief in something is no longer necessary because we know what is our Good. The idea that an ego or body can be connected to our Soul can only be delusional.

The ego is not part of our Soul. We cannot love, cherish or protect an ego in the way that our Good loves, cherishes and protects us. Our Soul is always connected to our Good. For this delusion to disappear to the nothingness from which it came, we focus our conscious mind on our superconscious mind of Good.

Our conscious mind has no ability to develop knowledge, but it can follow true knowledge of Good and deny all else. Our conscious mind cooperates only with our Good. We cannot throw away nor are we ever without our knowledge of Good. With knowledge of Good, we need no models, learning or study.

With knowledge from Good, there can be no surprise, disappointment or any other contradictory emotion. We cannot hurt ourselves nor is there any cause for our self-preservation. Our sacrifice is unnecessary nor do we have to give out of guilt in order to receive more later.

The instinct for fight or flight does not exist in our Good because there is nothing to attack or withdraw from. We cannot be threatened. We can neither be inflated nor deflated. The duality method of contrasting or comparing is not required in the realm of Good.

Our Soul cannot attack, reduce or destroy the concept of ego because ego is only a delusion that cannot occur in our Good. Ego cannot gain our Souls acknowledgment because the ego can only be perceived in the physical realm of time, space and matter. However, we cannot have delusions of the conscious mind because we are always connected with our Good. In our Good, we actually have no bodily or physical needs or appetites.

Our mind only has one channel, Good. With our knowledge of Good, we need not adhere to any erroneous thought system. Only facts, not conjecture, are in the realm of knowledge. Confusing realms of discourse are a thinking error. Our Good does not produce delusions or myths. Our Good is not ambiguous nor does it use innuendo. With our Good, we need not battle for survival. With our Good, there is no lapse in time. We are not autonomous.

Our Good has been attained therefore it is no longer necessary to discover how we have attained our Good. We cannot relate unrelated data, therefore all the data and knowledge of the physical universe cannot be related to the realm of Good. Scientists cannot measure the realm of our Good nor does their data from observing the physical realm have any validity.

The discoveries and conclusions of Psychology or other sciences cannot deliver our Good and are meaningless in the realm of Good. In our Good, we are never weak or deprived. With our Good, we do not need to work at self-esteem or confidence. We are always satisfied and need not prey upon others for our Good. We are harmless.

We cannot impose order upon the chaos of this world. Ingenuity and inventiveness can only be a wasted effort. With our knowledge from our Good, we need not explain anything. Our material science is not worthy of our knowledge of the immaterial realm of Good.

We are the Kingdom of Good. We have never left or been expelled. Our superconscious soul mind wills only our Good. The superconscious Soul mind can be our only reality. Our Good is perfectly united and never in danger. The physical shall never prevail against our Good. There can exist nothing beyond our Good.

We do not repress or judge our Good. The impulses from our Good can never be a threat. We are always in the presence of knowledge. We are totally conscious that there cannot be fear nor can there be anything in conflict with love. We can neither be inhibited nor do we need saving. Our Good is our guide. Truth contains no fallacy.

We are always conscious of our Good. There are no barriers to our Good. We do not own our Good but we are responsible for the maintenance of Good within our consciousness. An unconsciousness cannot exist. Life in the physical world is a paltry and meager mirage that can never prevail against our glorious gift of Good.

As we conceive our relationship with our Good we can only know love for ourselves. We have no enemies. We are permanent and steadfast. Human love can only be ambivalent. We desire and receive only true and meaningful love of our Good. We ask for and demand only for our continuous experience of glorious Good and Good answers us by showering Its grace upon us.

We have given up everything that opposes Good. There isn't a scrap of meanness left in us. The Light of Good has entered and expelled all the darkness of the physical universe. We are mindful of the love we receive from our Good. We require no other false gods or idols before our Good.

We explicitly ask only for our Good. Our Good remains in our Soul. We deny only that which opposes our Good. We have been given everything Good. Our Soul knows that we both have everything Good and are everything Good. We are never deficient of our Good. The calm being of the Kingdom of Good is perfectly conscious in our sane mind. The ego cannot win nor rule over sanity. We have chosen to hear only the voice of our Good.

We have willed to cooperate with our Good. The outcome of always receiving our Good is certain. Our real and lasting sense of abundance of Good allows for unending charity and generosity without fear or loss. We never do without our Good. We need do nothing except maintain our focus and enjoyment of our Good. Our Good provides us the vigilance necessary and our part is easy and effortless. We can never act or be insane.

We listen only to the voice of Good. Our attitude cannot be conflicted. Our feelings cannot be negative. Our behavior is never unpredictable or strained. We know where to look for ourselves and that is in our Good. We choose wisely and are always joyous. We only think correctly about the Souls created by our Good. We only think Good because our mind is one with Good. We are glorious creations which can never be depressed or deprived.

The capricious world of ego creates only anxiety and has no allure for us. We are always vigilant against capriciousness and rely totally upon the trustworthiness of our Good. Wrapped in the protection of our Good, we cannot sin. We have been created innocent therefore we can never experience guilt. We are above all delusions of temptation. We have risen above fatigue.

Our concentration and consistency with our Good is effortless. Our mind cannot slip away because we habitually and easily engage with our Good. We have permanently united our mind with our Good in everything we can think, hear, say or do. We have withdrawn our judgment, allegiance, protection and love from anything other than our Good. Our feelings are constant, satisfying and Good.

The Truth of our Good shines in perfect light where we never witness darkness. There is nothing to contrast with our Good. Our mind absorbs the eternal peace of Good knowing this and only this must be. Good shone upon us in our creation and brought our mind into being. We are transparent so that Good shines through us. Nothing can obstruct the light of Good.

Ego can never rule over our superconscious mind of our Soul. There is nothing that can exist in our mind that requires healing or restoration. Our Good works continually with our superconscious mind making it invincible. We do not need hope nor can we be confused. We have elected to keep our consciousness within the realm of the superconscious only. We cannot nor ever have experienced any form of insanity. All are knowledge and our thinking is sane.

All things work together for Good. There are no exceptions. The only impulses our body and mind can respond to are impulses from our Good. We need not fear the body or the conscious mind because it is always connected to our Good. The body is frail and the conscious mind cannot exist on its own.

To invest time and effort on the development of the body or conscious mind can only be a fool's errand, which can only isolate the conscious mind and body in meaningless nothingness. In this state both the body and the conscious mind are useless and can only foster nightmares of confusion.

Neither the body nor the conscious mind have any power or knowledge on their own. Alone the body and the conscious mind become fearful and threatened. The only sane answer is for the body and the conscious mind to turn and focus upon its Good. There lies our protection and security. The desire for our constant Good is our only desire.

Ego cannot be eternal. Ego would only lead us blindly desperately searching for something it cannot obtain. We are not in service to ego nor do we have the responsibility for its satisfaction and existence. Ego has no knowledge nor any favorable application. Ego can only keep the body and conscious mind in state of lack and wanting. Ego can only be deception from our Good that is not worth any amount of time, space or matter.

It is a waste to preoccupy the mind with insolvable problems. Our mind wastes no time or effort with what is nonessential. Our mind cannot be ill because our Good is clearly formulated and kept foremost in our mind. Our immortality is a constant state.

Everything Good is of great value. We want for nothing. Our Good is precise and perpetual. Trial and tribulation are not part of our Good nor can our perfect life experienced in our Good be interrupted.

We provide no allegiance to an ego. We do not follow direction from an ego. We do not exist in physical world of time, space and matter. An ego is only an erroneous thought about what we believe we are. To believe that we could exist in such a realm of confusion and chaos could only be labeled as a condition of disassociation from reality. We cannot live in an ego or act egotistically toward others.

We only receive natural impulses from our Good. Guidance comes only from our Good. We need not follow any other direction. We do not have any other choice but to choose peace and joy. Our rewards are eternal and sufficient. We have escaped any and all demands from such a limited source as an ego. We have no reasons to identify with an ego. We have no reason to humble, control, regulate or punish an ego.

We cannot disassociate ourselves from our Good. We demonstrate that we are not an ego. We are not nor could we ever be separated from our Good whereas the concept of I, ego, is a concept of separation, isolation and individualism. As we recognize our true relationship to one another, we are grateful for what our Good created. We are the Kingdom of Good.

We are grateful for one another. We experience our Good through one another. We collaborate with each other which is inherent in our prayer and meditation. We deliberately give forth our Good to one another.

All things are exactly as they are, Good. We value our Good. We share our Good. We do not disengage from our Good. Our Good envelopes us. We are immersed through and through with our Good.

We freely and rightly choose the presence and rewards of our Good. We associate joy to our Soul. We are always in complete and direct communication with every aspect of our Good. Our Soul responds to everything in the same way to everything It knows is Good and does not respond to anything else. However, our Soul does not establish what is not Good for there is no duality in our Good. Only misery can exist in the world of Good versus bad.

Because our mind is not material but naturally immaterial there can be no specificity that a material world represents. Our true existence cannot not be based upon concrete ideas. Our thought cannot come from concrete concepts related to sensation. A sane mind cannot depend upon the exclusive or peculiar.

Feelings and emotions are based upon limited but specific sensory input. Specificity creates the illusion of the material and the ego. Specificity can only disrupt our communication with our Good.

Good created our mind and Soul for communication. We are forever a receiver for the channel of our Good. As beings of like order, we communicate Good with one another. Our communication is perfectly abstract and universal in quality. Our communication cannot be subject to any judgement, any exception or any alteration.

We were created by Good. We were created by Communication for communication. Our mind has been designed solely for communication of our Good with our Good.

In the imaginary physical world of time, space and matter, it seems as if we are addicted to the sensations of our senses and emotions. However, we can immediately return to our Good by communication; which is speaking and listening only to our Good. We do this by keeping our mind in continuous communication with our Soul. We ensure that we are always aware of our glorious relationship with our Good. We do not desecrate or recoil from our true reality. Our home is the temple of our Soul.

Our Good is enjoyed more by communicating and sharing. Our creation is Divine abstraction applying joy throughout our experience and being. We are only created as individual beings to share our Good with others for the pleasure and joy of it.

In the realm of our Good there is no difference between having and being. In the state of being our mind continuously gives its Good. Our love is outgoing and cannot be blocked nor can its channels be closed. Our joy is always complete. There is no part split from our mind.

We know our Good with our whole mind. We reveal our Good because we are the owners of radiant light. As we are filled with Good and by default, we give praise and recognition to Good. Our Good rejoices through us. Our minds are truly cooperative with our Good. Every moment is an opportunity to gladden ourselves and make others happy. We naturally distribute our Good throughout our experience. Our joy calls forth our integrated willingness to share our happiness and promotes our mind's natural ability to respond as one.

Our beneficent thought is all the love and joy we have for one another. Our love and joy are the same. There can be no difference between the two. We are whole-heartedly happy. Love and fear cannot coexist. We completely deny any concept of fear as totally impossible. We are healed, forgiven and made wholly joyous as one. We know each other as we know ourselves.

Our natural impulse to give out our joy cannot be blocked. We are neither weak nor broken. We are in no need of rehabilitation or reform. Our body is not our temple.

We have been taught and we learned well all about our Good. Our Good is always helpful and it is we who represent our Good. Our Good directs us so that it is no longer our worry as to what to do or say in any situation. We experience our Good everywhere, always and now. We are content, satisfied, happy and free.

We are continually being blessed by our Good thoughts and actions. In gratitude we return our blessings. We love each other as we love our Good. We are gladdened as we know our oneness. We reveal pure joy.

Our minds can only obey the laws of Good. We honor only the laws of our Good. Our mind cannot choose to be something other than our Good. We have no need to acquire anything. The law that we follow is to give our Good forth. To Good getting is meaningless and giving is all. Having everything, our Good holds everything by giving it. Contrary to the physical world's laws, to give is not to lose anything. When we give forth our Good we do not lessen it, but instead our Good remains constant. It is a false association to connect giving with losing something.

We have invited in our Good and subsequently we give forth our thoughts of Good. The more who accept our gifts of Good the stronger and better our gifts become for those without their Good. Our Good is comforting and healing to those who seem to be without their Good. Our Good is our guide leading us to the locations where giving out our Good is most beneficial.

Our true Soul mind has the knowledge that lies beyond perception. Our true Soul mind has no need for healing and is never without comfort. The integrity of our true Soul mind is unquestionable and requires no restoration.

The universality of our Good is perfectly clear. Our Good is eternal and blesses us in the light of joy. Our Good has never allowed us to leave or separate from our Good. Our Good knows us only as Good therefore we can only know ourselves as Good.

Our Soul does not live in a physical realm of time, space and matter, but our conscious mind can grasp the Truth and can focus on our Good. Knowledge of our Good is the solution for the realm of time, space and matter. The knowledge from our Good dissolves all deluded perception of any chance of being separated from Good in any way at all. The perception of a physical realm of time, space and matter has never occurred, so there is nothing to let go or to be missed. There are no such things as the delusion of time, space or matter in our Good. The call of Good is all there is, whereas a call from ego in the reality of Good is nonexistent.

There is only one voice, the voice for Good. We tune our conscious mind to that Voice for Good and listen to no other sound. We hear the Voice for Good and no other. Our Good provides us undefeatable willingness. Our enterprise for Good is joyous, effortless and steadfast.

Because our Good is present, there can be no past or future. There never was a separation from our Good. There never was a time before or after a separation from our Good. Disassociation from our Good cannot occur. Having the knowledge from our Good we are in need of no guidance. We do not have the power to create anything other than Good. That is the only power that has been given to us by our Good. We can only use the Voice for Good. Any other voice is only a figment and can never provide us any Good. Any other voice could only be an powerless voice of deception and opposition to our Good.

Choice is meaningless in the realm of Good. There is nothing comparable to our Good. Our Good is not forced upon us, nor does it control us, but there is no sensible or sane reason to choose anything but our Good. Our Good cannot attack us nor do we need to defend ourselves against our Good. Our Good is quiet and speaks of peace.

Our devotion toward our Good cannot be mixed or divided with anything else. Our Mind is clear and explicit. We hear only one voice and that is the voice for our Good. We have chosen our Good and we have chosen to share our Good. We give our Good *as our Good is given to us. We are the light and we give forth light.*

We listen and call upon our Good and by doing so we exhibit strength of character. Our tasks are joyously based upon our equality with one another. We are always joined as one. Individuality or a self-centered ego has no place amongst our Good. We recognize one another as Souls created by our Good. We do not forgive, we give forth because we are unlimited and unhindered Souls. Our Good constantly transmits the knowledge we need for any given moment. We understand this through our experience of Good. Our Good is never lacking.

There is only one way that we can know each other. We see the Good in each other as we see the Good in ourselves. We are never weak in our mind or Soul. It is impossible to not hear our Good. We have given up an individual will and an individual ego. We neither fear nor produce fear. Time and delay are meaningless in eternity. We know and understand eternity perfectly. Eternity exists in our Good and Good exists in eternity.

Time is not a belief or a concept in our Good. We do not entertain interpretations from an individual and limited ego. We accept only the knowledge from our Good. As we look beyond symbols into eternity, we understand all the laws of our Good. We are holy and we are spirit. We require no interpretation or translation of our Good. Our one and only rightful place is in our Good.

We are poised and calm. Peace is our greatest ally. War, strife and attack do not exist in our Good and serve no purpose except to be an individual ego that wishes to gain it all. We already have it all and require no trinkets of deceit or delusion. Survival is not an issue nor do we need to compete to be the fittest. To believe in survival, strife, competition and war requires us to act viciously in order to protect ourselves from imagined danger, but danger is never a part of our Good. Nor does anything Good need protection from danger.

We cannot nor will we ever comprehend time or war because our mind cannot ever be split. Eternity and peace are closely interrelated. We are at home in eternal peace where there are no opposites. We are always in communion with our Good and we require no salvation. Good cannot be lost.

Only that which is loving can be true. Our loving thoughts are shared with every part of our Good. Our thought of Good keeps us forever free.

We could never be limited to an individual and limited ego nor can a limited and individual self keep us from our Kingdom of Good. A limited ego can only produce conflicting and limited thoughts. A limited self will attempt to blend opposite thoughts. We cannot be happy and sad, large and small, or alive and dead. We cannot share opposing thoughts or emotions. We share only our Good because our mind is Good and pure.

Our Good is always with us to provide us pure Good. Our Good provides us only pure thoughts without any contamination. We are whole and complete and cannot be hurt or destroyed. We treat each other as holy and Good.

A thinking system from an individual ego can only be insufficient and unsatisfying. An individual and limited ego can only provide contaminated thought. We hold nothing against ego because ego is nothing. There is nothing to resist or overcome. We cannot be both separate and complete.

From our Good, we receive our power to share our Good. The ideas from Good are never withheld. Our thinking of our Good is complete and lacks nothing. We are holy and cannot suffer. We receive our beauty, purity and blessings only from our Good and not from our own individual actions. We need not acquire anything. We are beyond destruction or guilt.

We do not side with the physical realm of ego. There is no guilt, shame or fear in the realm of our Good. Our decision to choose our Good was clear and easy. Our Good is truly blessed and can only give rise to joy. We are invulnerable to ego and our peace is unassailable. There is nothing that can disrupt our peace.

It is a meaningless concept to think that our Good could be attacked or that it needs protection. We do not believe or suffer any guilt in nonsense ideas such as we could possibly usurp our Good. To do so would only be pure insanity. Our guiltless mind cannot suffer or fear. We cannot project guilt into an external environment because there is no punishment to fear. Our Good can never be punishing or mete out any form of penalty or reprimand.

We only accept the reality of Good into our mind. We only think with our Good. As a result we are exactly like our Good. Our sane mind cannot conceive of illness. We cannot nor do we ever desire to attack anyone or anything.

We cannot eradicate our Good. We cannot oppose our Good nor can we interpret the laws of Good to satisfy material and self-gain. We have decided long ago that our Good can be our only alternative. This decision is unalterable. Our Good is irreversible and unchangeable.

We do not have to love an ego, for there is nothing to love. Neither do we have to love another's ego for that would be the same mistake. The delusion of ego is not real. Our Good could never be made up of an irrational and disordered ego. Our Good uses harmonious thought. We cannot feel guilt, lament or remorse. We cannot think apart from our Good. Good cannot be bereft. We are Souls with permanent and unshakable knowledge of our Good.

We think only Good, therefore we cannot have delusional thoughts. There is nothing to undo and we cannot undo nothingness. We have never entertained disordered thought. We do not believe in time, space or matter. We believe in the continuity of eternity and infinity.

There never has been nor could there ever be any judgment placed against us. With our Good we cannot be misled. There can be no vengeance or retribution from our Good. There is no part of our mind that can be turned over to or belong to an ego. Our thought cannot produce fear. Being or acting vicious serves no purpose.

We look only toward our Good. We require no patience or tolerance because everything is given to us in the now. We have no greed or selfishness because we give forth our Good as we have received our Good. There is only one voice that we hear which is the voice of our Good. There exists no other voice to listen to. We do not need hope because we already have everything Good. We have the infinite care and protection of our Good. We do not need faith because we already have all knowledge from our Good. We need no perform miracles because everything in our Good is miraculous.

Our will is always is accord with our Good. As Souls, we are completely sane. The spirit of Good has been commended to us as our Souls have been commended to our Good. We do not need to be healed because we are sane. Our Good cannot weep nor have any reason to be upset, therefore we never mourn nor are we disturbed. We are wholly joyous. We can never lack love because we are totally love. We cannot repent anything because our experience has always been perfect. There never was a time in which we could have erred. Error is impossible in our Good.

We cannot give thought to attack or fear. We cannot experience anger. We do not project separation from our Good. We cannot be attacked nor do we ever have any reason to retaliate. All our premises and conclusions are judicious and wise. Our sane thinking can only create sanity. Insanity cannot exist in Good. Our Good is what we teach to those who may have an illusion of an obstruction or impediment to their Good.

Our Good is the only worthwhile thought system. Anything else would only be undesirable and insane. Our allegiance is correctly placed in our Good. We accept our Good. We are incapable of insanity.

We are wholly devoid of fear. We are wholly benign. We can neither be punished nor tormented. We cannot be tortured or executed. We are never oppressed or persecuted. Nor could we ever commit any of these crimes and atrocities. These are extreme examples but there is no order of magnitude because none of these exist in our Good. A thousand times zero is still zero. Horror and holocaust never occurred nor could it in our Good.

We do not make foolish journeys into insanity. We give no attention to foolishness. Together with our Good we are invincible. We do not project anger or error into a physical world. We do not regard ourselves with anything destructive or perishable. Time, space and matter have no justification.

No one evaluates us. We are not judged. Evaluation and judgment in the terms of the physical world equate to zero. We have no reaction to any seeming form of evil. Evil equates to zero. We only exhibit perfect immunity to such illusion and delusion. We have no need to protect ourselves because we are unassailable. Our interpretation of all events and experience is Truth and Good.

In our Good, we cannot be rejected, betrayed or abandoned. We have no reason to defend our body or our ego. The love we receive from our Good has the power to keep us focused only upon our Good. We inspire love. The Good that we follow spares us any need for physical, emotional or mental pain. Any ostensible effect of ego is zero and meaningless in our existence in Good. They are only thinly veiled apparitions made on nothing and return to nothing. Erroneous thought creates the atom which appears to be real but in actuality has no real substance. The outrageous and the benign in a world of matter have no real substance.

Nothing of the world's judgments and evaluations concern our Good because they never really happened. History never happened. This world is no more real than the movies and television shows we watch. All the learning of the world's great universities equate to zero. All the atrocities of history equate to zero. Zero has no order of magnitude. Drama on any scale does not occur in our Good. Neither is there comedy or tragedy in the realm of our Good.

We have never been called upon to sacrifice in a world of insanity. We need not experience such a world to experience our Good. Our Good is infinity and also has no order of magnitude. It can only be continuously and consistently Good. We can neither experience a little nor a lot of Good. There is no duality in Good. We are not brothers and sisters; we are one. We are in a constant communication link with our Good that cannot be interrupted. We all know that we can neither hurt or be hurt. We demonstrate only love because that is what we are.

We have no use for weapons. We fear no wrath. We cannot project imperfect love. Anger or guilt are unknown and alien to us. Betrayal or condemnation are impossible. No Soul is ever punished for sin because sin does not exist. We are not sinners. Nor do we require adoration and indebtness. We have gratitude and appreciate only our Good.

Blame and punishment are unnecessary. We do not teach rejection. We are never at fault because we are connected and surrounded by perfection. Our will cannot be divided. Our whole mind recognizes and appreciates the indivisible wholeness of our Good. Omnipresence is all inclusive leaving nothing else. With the unconditional love of our Good, we could never be excluded or disowned. We are the same as our Good and have no reason to make ourselves safe. We are not of a physical world of unhappiness. We love one another inclusively. No one is special.

We know that we cannot find joy in a world that cannot comprehend what love actually is.

We are always where we think we are. We cannot be part of a complex delusion of nonreality. We are where our Good has placed us. We have total inclusion in our Good which is completely unalterable. We cannot change our Good into something less than Good. We deny everything which is not Good but we cannot deny our Good nor can we deny ourselves.

Our knowledge of our Good is perfect. There can be no counterpart to our Good. We are our Good therefore we do not need to be led to or meet our Good. We know our Good therefore we do not need to be taught what is our Good.

We live in and accept our Good. We cannot cross over into a realm of nothingness. Parallel realms do not cross over now, in the past or somewhere in the future. We know of no bridges that allows us to travel back and forth between realms as we please.

Reality of our Good cannot be reduced or bent into something mixed or opposed to our Good. In the realm of our Good, opposites cannot exist. There is neither duality or polarity in the realm of our Good. We know that physical laws cannot apply to the realm of our Good. All thought of our Good is perfectly united within our Good.

Our Good is complete and cannot be partially distributed. We are not apart therefore we cannot serve an individual self. We do not need to pray for ourselves or for our wellbeing because that is totally unnecessary and would be totally absurd. Such a concept of attempting to satisfy a self would be insane and naturally could never occur in our Good. Our prayer is the statement of our inclusion. Our purpose is to be our Good in all things.

Our Good cannot be projected or extended because our Good is omnipresent and encompasses all there is. Outside of the realm of our Good is nothing. Our joy is in our unitedness and unity. We neither create nor destroy. We cannot perceive anything because our thinking is not split. There are no multiple meanings or ambiguity for our Good. Perception of any kind is unnecessary. We are and can only be in Spirit and only Spirit is true.

Our mind is Spirit. Our mind is sanctified in our Good. We need not correct or restore our mind to sanity. We have never been separated from our Good. An individual ego in a physical world never has occurred nor will it ever occur. We cannot experience problems. We cannot experience the physical because the physical does not exist. Our mind is in direct communication with our Good.

We are permanently joined with our Good. We are every mind. We see only ourselves. We see only Good. The peace of Good lies within us and shines in our mind forever. We are legion and we are one. Only Good abides within us. We need not surrender anything.

Imagination cannot serve us, but keeps one in never ending loops of obstructed awareness of our Good. Every concept, idea, image, memory, invention or fantasy is part of an endless series of interlocking meanings and nuances of unending complexity. There is no line between true versus false, good versus bad, acceptable versus unacceptable, desirable versus objectionable, etc. Such a limited, contradictory and endless stream of mental babble can only overwhelm and drown a seeker. Such a system allows one to seek but to never find. This worldly system produces an endless proliferation of data to obfuscate our Good.

We are not part of an experience that feeds into continuous interlocking loops that propagate further loops. We do not involve ourselves in attempting to undo a kaleidoscope of imaginings. We do not enlist ourselves into an impossible project of purification from voluminous, expanding, surreal imaginings. We simply remain focused upon our Good and reject and deny all linear and dualistic properties of perception. We invest no thought or energy into such nonsense. Rather than quantity we focus upon quality.

We neither own our mind nor do we create its content. We are not the thoughts, feelings, images and memories of a physical world. The misconception that it is necessary to group our thoughts into purposeful categories to create and maintain an illusion of an individual self is futile and fruitless. We neither need to create a collection and structure of thought processes nor do we need to protect it. We do not allow any linear, dualistic and imaginary construction to deny us our Good.

We know that ideas and concepts do not have any significance or importance in our Good. We know that there are no dividing lines or opposites in our Good. We are neither the author nor the owner of our thought or our mind. There is no value in ownership or authorship of singularity. In our Good, we need not control our thought or secure its survival. Thought does not represent an individual self. We do not own our mind, therefore to have a misconception that it is "my mind" is insane.

We need not spend years surrendering to nonsense to discover we are no further along than whence we began. We do not attempt to surrender content of imaginings as fast as it seems to be produced. We do not attempt to detach from something that does not exist. We do not believe that individual mental content will bring happiness or solve problems. To believe that our individual thinking is a road to success, wealth and happiness is only an empty promise. We do not believe that we are the source of our protection and survival. We have no need to fear loss of self-identity because we cannot be unique or special as individual personalities. We are enamored with our Good and not our self.

We do not cling to thought of disaster, pain, failure or suffering for we know such things cannot exist in our Good. There is only love that can exist in our Good and there can be no opposite or mixture of love with opposites such as hate, dislike, contempt, etc. In our

Good there are no negative emotions. In our Good there is no requirement for martyrdom or victimhood; and there can be no satisfaction from a grim justification for pain and worry.

We have no reason to be in love with our thought, emotion and perception of this physical world and body. We need not defend or make excuses for nonsense. Jealousy, envy, guilt, punishment and hatred are nonsense. It is nonsense to become infatuated with a glamorized image of an individual self. As well it is nonsense to look out into a physical world for objects to love and attach to. Physical objects or bodies cannot bring permanent internal happiness. Our Good does not allow us to fear or grieve the loss of anything physical because the physical is only a falsely created illusion of electromagnetic fields. Thought and emotion can be totally dispensed with because they are only an interference with our Good. We are in love with our Good and not our thinkingness.

We cannot attach ourselves to an imaginary physical world and body so there it is needless to fear its loss. Only Good is attached to our existence. There is no individual or personal subject or object. Our totality is held in our Good. Our Good is always present but cannot be experienced individually because It is a nonlinear all-encompassing field of awareness and love.

Laws of physics are imaginary based upon perception, therefore they do not exist. If there is no matter then there are no three dimensions of matter or space. We do not observe from a center point with a radius outward. Time does not come at us wearing things down and aging us. Light cannot be expanding and traveling into a realm where there is no light. There is no motion, friction or gravity. There are no lines, geometry or mathematics in the nonlinear.

We cannot experience a limited or permanent life in an impossible universe. We only and always experience the completely different realm of Good. This realm requires no imagination nor does it require us to create laws, rules or regulations. In the realm of

Good, we are conscious and aware but the neither the impossible nor the possible occur. Extremes of duality cannot be real in a realm of nonduality. Linear mathematics or physical laws cannot apply to a nonlinear realm. Laws of time and space do not apply to a realm of eternity and infinity. Individual or groups of egos, ambition, competition, greed, self-centeredness, etc. cannot occur. Belief in an ego or ideas and concepts created by an ego cannot be created or carried over into the realm of Good.

Our Good is unconditional and is not subject to opinion, attitude or laws. Our Good loves us because that is our essence. Our Good is not earned or subject to limitation. There is no border or division between us and our Good. There is no polarity between a self and our Good. Good is beyond duality and conditions.

We need do nothing to receive our Good. It is already here and now. We are always aware of our Good. There are no obstructions to be dissolved. There is no need for any form of surrender for we never have been defeated. We are and have always been spiritual beings of our Good.

There are no barriers to our communication with our Good. We cannot be threatened or defiled. An individual ego never was and could never be part of our Good. We neither learn nor teach what is not true. There is no bad, wrong or unfair. There isn't anything that deserves punishment. There is no error therefore there can be no accident nor can anyone or anything be at fault. There is no falsehood to recognize and comprehend.

A physical world cannot cause innocent to suffer. There are no wicked. Everyone wins so there is no need for competition. There are no wrongs that need to be righted. Our Good prevails and perceptions are meaningless.

An individual ego or a group of egos will never be part of our Good. It is futile to believe otherwise. Trying to learn and teach what is not true in a physical world is a waste. It is denigrating to *teach and believe we are something that we actuality are not. We are not the antithesis of knowledge. We have nothing to question. There is nothing to gain from conflict. It is ineffective to deny our love and rightful inheritance.*

We are gentle and harmless. We are perfectly safe and wholly benign. The blessing of our Good irradiates. We have no reason to experience anxiety. Our mind is wholly kind and we illuminate beneficence. We have nothing to compromise. Attack can only work against itself.

Our knowledge of our Good is immortal and it is impossible to disassociate from our Good. We cannot throw away our Good. We share only Good.

An individual ego can only be capricious and create ill will. An ego can neither create nor find love. Ego is loud and boisterous. Ego can only be a thinking malfunction. We will never be without love therefore the concept of an existence of a loveless ego is erroneous. However we cannot doubt what we truly are; which can only be Good.

We are not a human body with a mind and sensory devices. Therefore we have no alliance with it nor do we ally with fear. We never ally with any form of separation from our Good. There is no conspiracy of an ego and body attempting to corrupt our Good. We are always in our right mind and the unreal provides no attraction. We cannot be tempted. We never consider such foolish persuasion that there is anything more real than ourselves.

We instantly know the answer for any useless question and dismiss it accordingly. We require no ideas. We will always be part of the priceless kingdom of our Good. Nothing else exists and only our Good is real. We neither sleep nor have dreams. We are continuously spiritually awake. We cannot be confused. We neither believe in dreams nor take action to make dreams come true. We can only be beautiful and true.

We are certain that we are Good and only Good. We have never lived in the questioning dream. We know only eternity and infinity. Our proficiency is certain and our skill is for the certainty of our Good. We are immersed in our Good so we need not escape from or get out of anything. We have no reason to perceive that we are enslaved. We have no reason to perceive duality... to perceive right or wrong, good or bad, up or down, positive or negative, etc.

We could never find ourselves in an impossible situation. We are aware of only our perfection. We are neither helpless nor inadequate. We cannot be insulted. We never command because to do so would assume inequality. We never control because to assume control is inequity. Our Good is constant. We are faithful only to our Good. Our Good would never condemn us to sin. Our Good has no reason to frighten us.

There is nothing to teach with our omniscient Good. There is no lack in the knowledge of our Good. Our Good is changeless. We can neither lose our perfection nor can we ever fail to communicate with our Good. We cannot be taught wrongly nor can we believe in what is not true. Our Good imparts Its joy to Its entirety. A spiritual awakening is unnecessary because we never have nor could we ever be asleep and unaware of our Good. Our Good's sharing with us cannot be blocked. There is no night or dark in our Good. We need not be afraid of dreaming.

We are now and always have been safe in our Good. We never have any reason to avoid or escape from. It is simple and perfectly clear for us to do only Good. We do not confuse our reality with fantasy. We speak of only what lasts forever. Nothing is accomplished through death. We are life eternal. Our life is of our Soul and Superconscious Mind. The body neither lives nor dies. There is no body, therefore there is no part outside the body nor is there anything within a body, whether it be physical or spiritual. The body does not contain the Soul or the

Superconscious Mind. We share the same Good and never have to overcome death or ignorance.

The concept of a body like the concept of this planet and universe is that they are destructible, therefore these imaginings are not of the Kingdom of Good. This realm of physical experience cannot exist in Good, therefore it is nothing. There is no device that could separate us from our Good. Only our Good can be shared and our Good can only be shared with our unified Soul and Superconscious Mind. Everything else is meaningless and nonexistent. We are perfect equality. We experience only full appreciation for one another. There are no scales, ranges or orders in our Good. There is no difficulty whatsoever. There is no more or less in our Good.

Our communication with our Good is our being. We have no reason to use a body for attack, defense, greed or pride. We do not communicate fear or loss. Communicating fear promotes attack which breaks communication which is not only insane but impossible. We have infinity and eternity so we can give infinitely and eternally, but there is no point in giving or receiving.

There is never any conflict in turning toward and receiving our Good. We never accept conflict or competition as an alternative to our Good. Our Good would never reject or abandon us. We have no reason to fear any form of retaliation or retribution. We emit only our Good. Disassociation from our Good is impossible as is projection of maleficence or malevolence. In our Good, insanity cannot occur. Since we have total knowledge of our Good, we cannot be taught nor can we teach maleficence or malevolence. We share only our Good. Our motivation needs no strengthening.

We do not have to give because everyone we encounter has everything as well. Nothing needs to be undone. Nothing needs to be obtained. We never change our mind from our Good. We are consistent with our Good and never encounter any contradiction. We entirely trust our fellow Souls and have no reason to ever doubt their validity. Being and having are the same thing within the Kingdom of our Good, a place we have never departed. There is never any task that is difficult or cumbersome. We joyously experience Good easily and effortlessly. Challenge cannot occur in the realm of our Good because there is no duality.

The voice of Good is always clear and specific. We listen only to the voice of our Good. There is no other voice. There is only one thought system and that is the thought system of Good. Conflict and competition can only be insane and anything insane cannot exist within our Good.

There can be no conflict between insanity and sanity because there is no such thing as insanity in a world of consistent Good. There are no such things as decisions because there is only our Good and no other choice. We are not asked to make decisions because there is only Good which has no degrees.

We represent peace. We illuminate our Good. Desirable has no degrees. Our vigilance comes from our Good and we are vigilant only for our Good. All exists in our Good therefore nothing needs to be created or destroyed. We require no salvation. The Kingdom of Good remains in our mind at full strength and there is nothing that can weaken it. There is no falsehood that needs to be separated from our mind. We are now and always in accord with our Good. Purification is unnecessary. Our Good is perfectly consistent and unified.

There is no fundamental disagreement with our Good from a nonexistent ego. An individual ego can only be illusory in the realm of Good. There is no disagreement about what we are because we can only be Good and nothing else exists. There can be no doubt in what we are in the realm of Good. We are Good. The only mood we engender is Good. We are wholly joyous. Being wholly in the present there is no past or future, therefore there are no memories, lament, remorse or desires in our Good.

We are never critical of other Souls. There is no requirement to either strengthen or weaken a singular self. We neither possess a singular self nor does any other entity. We have no use for judgment in the only realm that can exist. We can only be vigilant for our Kingdom of Good. Fundamental change is unnecessary because the rudiments of our Good are intact, whole and complete. We need not be vigilant against anything. In our Good there is no dichotomy between desirable and undesirable. It is inconceivable and impossible to choose anything but our Good. There is no direction we could travel that would be unsatisfying or fearful.

We are so empowered by our Good, that we could never be enslaved by an individual ego that needs to survive and compete in a limited world of time, space and matter. We are spiritual and have no use for an imaginary individual will. We neither live in a world of form nor do we follow any laws from such a façade. Our consciousness is far superior to such insanity that there is nothing left to entice us into such a deplorable existence. Our awareness and insight from our Good shows us the folly of desiring an individual ego.

The unconscious cannot exist in our realm of consciousness of our Good. In our Good, there is nothing that needs forgiveness. Compassion is a constant state of our Good. We are beyond any limitations of time, space or matter. We are and always will be in the nonlinear realm of Good. Whatever we desire to accomplish is without strife, struggle, or sacrifice. Our realm of Good is unquantifiable.

An ego could never be our enemy nor would we ever have any desire to attack and defeat an ego or egos. We have absolutely no use for the trappings of guilt, shame, criticism, condemnation, avoidance, rejection, etc. We require no tools for survival. In our Good we naturally fit into our society without conflict or judgment. In our Good, there is no persona or need for intellectual development.

Chaos and consistency cannot coexist. However in the realm of our Good, exclusivity and inclusivity are identical. There are no choices in our Good. Our mind is filled only by our Good. In our Good having, receiving and giving are all one. We cannot lose or gain so there is no motive or fear. We neither learn nor teach so there is no ambition. We are never without. We neither exclude nor include. We are beyond belief; we are beyond question. There is no doubt because our oneness is assured by our immeasurable Good. We are not divided into separate parts. We are connected and whole. We are now, have been and will always be aware of only our Good.

Although we communicate fully with our Good, our relationship is not reciprocal because we did not nor do we now create our Good nor can we alter or destroy our Good. Our power only comes from our Good and all that we can desire or experience can only be Good. Good is not contained by boundaries, therefore it can neither expand nor contract. Good permeates all.

Infinity and eternity are ours and all experience is Good. Eternity and infinity can only be filled with Good, therefore we need make no deals or bargains with our Good. We need not demand reciprocal rights because we are equal to each other and with our Good. There is nothing to gain or increase. We need not give or take anything but our Good. Our will can only be Good.

There is no beginning nor an end to our Good. There can never be any imperfection in our Good. There are no steps or procedures to follow to obtain our Good because we are never without our perfect Good. Good will allow and then deliver us from any and all experience. Good will forever entertain us as well as keep us entertained.

Our Good does not come gradually nor is it measured by gradients. Our Good is timeless and changeless. There is nothing to accomplish or obtain because our Good is always, everlasting and permanent. We do not receive our Good by following stepwise procedures. Our Good is instantaneous. There is neither a beginning nor an end, nor is there a first and last that pertains to our Good.

Our Good is never obscured and is always shared with us. We can never be sick or think that we are ill in any form. We cannot envision anything as diseased. We are whole and never lack or are in need. We cannot see anyone or anything absent of our Good. We cannot separate ourselves from our Good nor can we leave the Kingdom of our Good. We have no need to correct perception because our Good is unified and integrated. Our thought always comes from our Good. We obey our Good by default because there is no other way. We joyously obey. Obedience to our Good is a joy and never a burden or a choir.

We need not fight for or defend our freedom because it comes abundantly and naturally. We have always been given freedom just as we always side with our Good. We have no reason to listen to conflicting voices that provide diametrically opposed outcomes. We are free from such nonsense. With the knowledge provided by our Good we cannot be misguided. Because we are not individual egos, there can be no interpersonal nor intrapersonal conflict. We are in perfect accord with the mind of Good.

We are not separate nor are we bounded by a body. We are not geometric form nor do we have dimensions of width, depth and height. We are not bound by law. We have no beliefs nor do we perceive or project thought. The mind of Good is in perfect accord and there is only certainty. We require no teaching, learning or education. We are surety of being. There is no outside the Kingdom of our Good therefore there are no procedures that must be followed to return.

There are no different languages as there are no blocks or hindrances to communication with our Good. We need no translator. The meaning of our Good cannot be changed or misinterpreted. Our Good and the meaning of our Good is constant. Our mind cannot be conflicted nor can we create multiple meanings for something that is always constant. We are always faithful to our Good. We have no need to preserve the form of anything and our Good is always and constantly preserved.

We require no communication, translation or interpretation of law because there is only Good without law, rules and regulations. There are no meaningful differences to our Good. Differences pertain to duality and do not exist within our Good. Good does not require truth versus false. The only truth is that Good is ours. We could never be disinherited or disowned by our Good.

We have no need for learning or memory in our Good. There is nothing for us to relinquish or forget. Forgiveness is unneeded. There is no confusion to intermingle with meaning. The communication from our Good is perfectly direct and consistent. We are perfectly united in our Good. There is never strain or discordance.

We are the will of our Good and our identification with our Good is not optional because Good is what we are. We do not have to decide anything. In reality, we can neither experience separation from our Good nor can we experience fallacy. Our true Good is not open to choice. All Good has already been given to us by our Good. We cannot undo that. We are and will be always left in comfort. We can never be confused about what we are. We are love, joy, health, sanity, truth, etc. Living our Good is easy and effortless. We are forever guided and entertained by our Good

We are not of this physical world because the world of time, space, energy and matter are imaginary and temporal. The physical realm is contrary to our true nature which is Good. In reality, there are no orders of difficulty. Our natural state is always in the state of grace. Our natural state is to be always happy and satisfied.

Our Good is our worth. Our worth is beyond measure. Our home is in our Good. Our Good protects us from fear and shines love into our hearts. Our Good provides us gratitude and appreciation. Our Good is the only environment in which we exist and our Good keeps us happy in our existence.

We do not make Good, but we do share it. We share our love from Good with everything we encounter. Our mind knows only Good. There is nothing that needs to be healed. Our radiance shines and darkness cannot exist. We recognize, know and appreciate the majesty of our Good. We know and experience equality. We know ourselves and our Good intimately. We have been created by Good to experience only Good which is the only Truth that there can be. All else is a lie.

The majesty of Good is recognizable and available to know and appreciate. Our inheritance is accepting our Good. Our Good is provided to all equally. As we see the Good in others we recognize our own inheritance. Good is easy to perceive. We immediately, clearly and naturally know that our Good is the only Truth there can be.

We know ourselves as we know our Good. We know our Good as we know our ourselves as equally Good. There is nothing to heal. Our brothers and sisters stand before us as perfect creations of Good. We do not deny Truth or any part of Truth. Creator and Creation are one which is Good. We instinctively know the Good of all of creation in which we are all united as one.

Our reality of Good has been established and is invincible. Our Good is shared. To know our Good is to know all Creation. We have been given peace and knowledge, therefore there is no need for motivation. And since we are peaceful, we have no need for conflict and experience it not. There is no need to restore our knowledge or our peace. Our allegiance is always with our Good.

We neither believe in an ego nor do we give away our power for Good to anything but Good. Since there can only be Good within our mind, there is no need to remove anything. We cannot give up our knowledge or peace no more than we can give up our Good. Since we have all encompassing knowledge, we need not learn anything nor do we have any need to change. Since we have no need to learn, we have no need for a curriculum or an Atonement.

In our Good, our mind cannot be split nor can our happiness be taken. In our Good, we do not entertain confusion. A "nothing" cannot exist, therefore a "nothing" cannot interfere with our Good. We are without motivation, therefore we have no desire to leave our Good for "nothing".

Our Good is never coercive because our Good is gentle. Our voice is in agreement with our Good. Our Good is boundless. All things are in the realm of our Good, therefore there can be only nothing else. We are the will of our Good, so there is only "Good Will", not "free will". We cannot choose "nothing" as an alternative to our Good. We are the boundless power and glory of our Good.

All the power and glory of Good is ours as well. And that glory and power is without limit. In the spiritual realm, Good has one direction and that direction is always freedom. This freedom is joy and happiness.

We have no need for a Holy Spirit to restore us to the Kingdom of Good. We could not nor never have chosen anything but our Good. We need not be called to our Good because we are always within our Good. We are awake and aware of our Good which runs easily and gladly though the endless Kingdom of Good.

We need not ask for anything to be given to us, because we already have. We are equal to our Good and have no needs, nor should we have any desires. We are satisfied and content in our Good. We understand all things. Our mind and our knowledge is limitless so we have no need for more understanding. We have no need for more enlightenment or more light. The will of Good is not forced upon us because we were created equally with our Good and force cannot affect us. Our willingness for Good is always an invariable constant, yet that constant is always infinity.

In our Good, there is no place for someone to teach someone else for we all have the same infinite knowledge. By being created in Good equally, there can be nothing superior or inferior. We fulfill the will of Good perfectly. It is the only experience possible. We are always willing to experience our Good so there can be no contention that we could lack willingness, for we lack nothing.

There is no need for a Holy Spirit, for we never left nor could we ever leave our Good. There is only one Truth, not two. We are one with our Good. This is perfect creation, perfectly created in union with perfect Good. Our Good is all that there is; there is nothing else. That is the only Truth there can be. Everything is Good and nothing else can exist. There is no need to extend Good because it already encompasses everything. Therefore, meeting one another can only be a Holy encounter where Good encounters Good.

To "know Thy Self" is not a mystery. You are Good and you can only experience Good, because that is all there is. There is nothing else but Good to experience. You cannot be misled, deceived, blinded or insane. You are not lost nor have you ever lost your Good. Your power and glory from Good cannot be defiled. Our place in the realm of Good is equally united and steadfast. We are never alone nor do we have to seek for anything. The dominion of Good does not need to be found nor do we need to be found.

Our Good which is everything is everywhere. Our strength and power is in our Good. We cannot suffer. We can never choose incorrectly because our Truth is perfection everywhere now. There is no power from any other source. Wrong decisions are an impossibility. There is nothing that needs to be undone. We can only experience the glory of Good.

Our knowledge does not establish a place for forgetfulness. We have no need to remember anything. We are constantly aware of all that is Good and we have nothing to forget. We know that we are Good and there is nothing else to remember. To think that there is something to remember that we have forgotten and to apply effort to remember what that is can only be a fool's errand, yet there are no fools in the realm of our Good. We are not ignorant of anything and we cannot be fooled.

There is nothing we can give to another because they already have all. There is nothing wrong with anyone else we may perceive. They can only be perfectly Good. We have no need for judgment, protection or correction.

Our Good has provided us with imagination, a vast realm of potentiality. But our Good could never provide us with anything that would not be in our best interests for Good. Eternity is vast and infinite therefore we can never reach any position of limitation. And Good cannot be usurped. Unconditional Love will never be denied us. There is no special action we must take to receive the unconditional love from our Good.

We are and will always be united in our Good. There is no opposite to Good. We need not renounce anything. There is no need for transcendence from perfection. We have never left the peace of our Good. Nothing prevails over our Good.

We all already know the will of our Good. Fear has no real power over our Good. There are no entities separate from our Good that can sense, think or deceive. There is no ego that needs to be defeated. There can be nothing that is against us. We are invulnerable. Nor do we require another force or entity to aid us or save us from the Bogeyman.

There is no power that can interfere with our Good and there are legion of Good that are always available to ensure our Good. There is only one Truth and no other or opposite. There is nothing other than Good in which we can give our power to. We never leave our Truth behind. Although we may use illusion and imaginings for entertainment, we are never really separated from our Good.

We want for nothing. We neither gain nor lose strength. We have no weakness that needs to be laid aside. Our Good is with us always and not waiting somewhere for our return. Being equal with our Good, we need not glorify or worship any other entity. There is only Good, above, below and around us. We are eternal, infinite and immortal and we can be deprived of nothing.

There isn't a duality where one thing is Good and another is bad. There is only Good. Our Good cannot be limited to certain conditions or circumstances.

We need not give anything to anyone because they already have. We need not receive anything because we already have it all. Creation is complete and needs no further extension. Our Good does not need to be extended to others nor could we actually accomplish such a task. Our Good is eternal and infinite, so how could we accept anything else.

Our Good does not require our devotion. Our Good demands nothing from us. Our Good does not require us to be remorseful. We need not do anything for we always remain in our Good.

Our Good has no gender for our Good encompasses all. There is only one order of reality. Our mind cannot be blocked nor can we ever be ill. Our mind continuously communicates our Good and only our Good. We are always joined in the communication of our Good. The mind cannot be arrested because we only listen to our Good. We are always in good health. Our thought cannot be made flesh. We are not a body therefore we can never be limited by a body.

Good is unified purpose. Our purpose is always unified with our Good. We are never condemned nor can we condemn ourselves. We know that we are not matter. We neither suffer nor can we imagine suffering. Our mind is free to imagine all forms of Good. Our Good is continually extended to us. We are limited in only Good and we cannot have any other experience, but our communication with Good is unlimited.

Health is continuously provided by our Good. We cannot experience any limitation to our Good. We cannot believe otherwise. The function of our body is to experience Good. Our Good never changes and is permanent. Our mind has only one voice and that is the voice of Good. We cannot experience confusion. The mind and the body are in the divine perfect order of Good. We are always content and satisfied. There is nothing that we need to achieve or succeed. There is nothing that we need to hope for because we have received all in our Good.

In our Good, we are invulnerable. Sickness is never an option. We need not put any effort into defense against sickness or attack. Our mind and body only serve our Good and cannot be judged for they are always in divine perfect order. We cannot be attacked physically or microbially. There is only one function of the mind and body, which can only be Good; our body and mind cannot experience misfunction.

There is no need to judge the experience of our mind and body. We are much more than the experience of the mind and body. We are the experience of our Good, therefore the experience of the mind and body can only be Good.

We cannot be sick or be hurt. We are never frail in our Good. Our guidance and substance come from our Good. We do not need prescriptions, medicines, surgery or treatment for illness. As we are in our Good there can be no catastrophe. We never need to handle error.

The realm of science is totally unnecessary as is the need for data. Nothing needs to be complicated. Complication is nothingness. We neither need to be taught or guided. We cannot accept confusion as part of our reality in our Good.

There is only one way to feel and that is to feel Good. Only knowledge of our Good has being. A voice for Good cannot come from nothing. We cannot be misdirected. There is no ego that needs to be laid aside. Our freedom of choice only lies within our Good. There is no other choice but Good. We are not sick nor do we need to be healed. Our mind can never be split. We cannot perceive littleness. Health of body and mind is our only state of being. We cannot opt to use our mind or body lovelessly. We are constantly immersed and filled in the love from our Good. There is only one life and that is the life of Good. Cosmic vibration is Good.

With the knowledge of Good we have no questions therefore we need no answer. We have access to the knowledge of everything. And what we know is Truth. There is only one Truth which is that our Good is constant, continuous and here, now. We are never wrong nor could we ever perceive incorrectly. There is only one true reality and that reality is harmless.

Our Good never provides us challenges nor tests us. Our Good never asks of us for perseverance through difficult situations. Our Good never places fear in our path and there is never anything to fear in our Good. We neither sleep nor dream. We do not need to be awakened. We are always awake in our joy and happiness. We are always at ease in the peace of our Good.

We are never separated from our Good. Our mind or body cannot be weak or exist separated from our Good. We are always perfect, without error and completely whole in our Good. We need not accomplish anything. We cannot withdraw from our Good. We limit ourselves to be of one mind, the mind of our Good. We are unified in purpose. Our existence has significant meaning. Our Good stands forever in all things.

To believe that we have a free will that could do harm to ourselves or others is absurd and would be an atrocity as well as an impossibility. Atrocity is nonexistent in our Good. Our will is only for our Good. It is equally impossible to fear our Good. Reality only upholds Truth and our Truth is that we cannot fear anything. Our knowledge is comprehensive and we are totally aware. There is nothing hidden from our Good. We have no need for a guide to lead us out of darkness because in our Good there is no darkness.

Our will for Good cannot be hindered or imprisoned. Nothing exists beyond our awareness. There is no need to sort or eliminate anything from our mind. We cannot hide things from our Good. We constantly know who we are and have no need for memory. We can never lose anything that has been given to us by our Good. There is never a need to sacrifice or give up any part of our Good. And we need not be saved.

Our communication with our Good always functions in divine perfect order. There is nothing lost in translation and there is never miscommunication or misunderstanding with our Good. We never have any reason to question our Good for our Good is satisfying, constant and sustaining. We are always safe in the reality of our Good. Our will can only be Good and we could never do wrong. There can be no difference or degrees of Good nor can our will ever be opposed to our Good. Nor are we ever alone. We cannot be abandoned by our Good.

There is no death in our Good nor is there anything to fear. Everything has been created and it is all Good. More creation is unnecessary and impossible. Our will is always one with Good. There are no heretics, atheists or martyrs. We all believe in our Good. We are always in the security of our Good where fear is totally meaningless. Good is the only cause and Good creates love, peace and safety and not fear, anxiety or apprehension. Our peace, safety and love belong to us. It is our inheritance from our Good.

There is nothing that can hurt us therefore we cannot ask for anything other than our Good. We need never ask for anything because our Good in infinite and eternally here and now. And our Good will never fail to recognize us. We always readily accept our Good. We can neither deny nor change our Good. Laws of happiness are ours always. We have no need for goals or objectives. Our devotion can only be centered in our Good and our Good is devoted to us. There are no orders of reality that oppose our Good.

Our Good is the only reality possible. There is nothing else that could ever be. The reality of our Good cannot be distorted therefore anxiety, depression and panic are impossible. Good is always in us and we are always Good. We need not pray in supplication for our gratitude is eternal. Nor do we need to escape from fear. We express Good, mind, body and soul. We hear, know and express Good continually without interruption. And we always know that we are Good. We shine of the light of Good. Our faith is without question or disruption. There is no other Truth and we have absolutely no ability to entertain a lie.

We all hear our Good. We can neither deceive or be deceived. Nor do we have to pay a price for anything. We can only believe in one another and there can be no judgment. We do not need anything, therefore we do not have to get or buy anything. We all have everything, so there is nothing to trade. All Good is of equal value. We appreciate all of our Good in its various forms.

We all receive our Good equally. There are no degrees of Good. One never has more or less than another. We need not want, get or give away anything. All things are of equal value because all things are Good. We have all of Good available to us in the present moment. We can only see Good in ourselves for there can be no evil. Error is impossible with our Good therefore we never need correction.

We can see no error for we cannot err. Nor can we judge anything or establish a certain value to it for all things are equally Good. And since we cannot judge, we cannot react. Since we know only Truth we cannot perceive. Nothing requires correction. Insanity can never be a choice for us nor could we perceive insanity in anything else; for everything is perfectly Good.

We have everything Good so there is nothing that we need to give over to be changed or corrected. We do not teach nor do we need to be taught. We cannot condemn anything. We neither correct ourselves or others. We always readily accept our Good. We have no power to perceive and then react to error as if it were real. We will never lose our way so we do not need to find our way either. We cannot accept error as real. Without error, nothing requires forgiveness nor atonement.

Forms of error, such as arrogance are an impossibility for we are Good. We neither believe in error nor evil. Good does not need correction. We neither correct Good nor create Good for it is, has been and will always be Good. Our purpose is not to create but to enjoy our Good.

We are never alone nor is anything designed for singular enjoyment. It is impossible to enjoy alone. There is no selfishness so we could never experience it. We all are unified in Good. There is no error and there is no need for correction nor for a guide or teacher. We all have and never need to share. We have only but one nature and that is Good. Good is natural for us.

We need no plan for forgiveness. We cannot perceive anything meaningless or unreal. We never forget our Good. All of our ideas come from our eternal knowledge of Good. What does not exist cannot affect us. There is no reason to prove that nothing does not exist and we know how to fulfill our Good perfectly. We do not need to learn how to perform this function nor do we have any reason to react to nothingness.

We do not require salvation therefore we do not need a teacher for salvation. Anything representing itself as a guide must be insane and can have absolutely no effect upon us therefore we could never detect another as a guide or teacher with more knowledge than which we already have. We can never think, act or feel insane in our Good and we always choose Good.

There is not an ego. An ego cannot exist. It is impossible for an ego to live within us. An ego cannot be an evil bogeyman that must be resisted. We have never left our Good and we can never be insane. The word ego is meaningless and equates to nothing. Nothing cannot have a negative significance. Nothing has no meaning nor effect. Nothing cannot cause or create.

We know reality implicitly and have no need to change our mind about reality. Our Good is our reality. We are never wrong living in our Good.

We neither live in the past nor the future. The past and the future are unreal as well. We have no requirement for memory or fantasy. We do not create for all Good has been created. Our only function is to enjoy Good that has been created for our enjoyment and entertainment. Even when our mind is using memory or fantasy, we are still always in the mind of our Good. We do not need to search our fantasies for truth.

Nothing can have a plan for forgiveness because forgiveness is unnecessary. The only use for forgiveness is in fantasy and memory and it is always used for Good. We are never miserable. We cannot sin. We have no need for healing nor do we have to give or receive anything. We always know Truth.

In our Good, we are neither a body nor a mind, therefore, Good cannot attack or harm, and we cannot attack, harm, be attacked or be harmed. Fear does not exist in our Good so we need take no action to reduce fear. In our Good we are never confused. We waste no time analyzing nothingness or acknowledging darkness. There are no dark corners or obscure vagaries in our Good. We are real and we cannot be denied our Good.

We all have the same amount of Good to give or share so that giving and sharing are meaningless. No one needs correction. No one needs anything for we are all provided for in our Good. We see clearly in the light of Goodness. In our Good, we have complete understanding of all that is Good and know of nothing but Good. We do not believe in nightmares or impossible situations.

We are not traveling or destined to anywhere for we are in right place. We need no direction or journey. We have no questions. We see only light. We know only Goodness. Our dreams are Good. We have no need for miracles for our mind is always correct and sane. Only Good speaks through us and only Good sees perfection and beauty in all things. From Good we know ourselves. We are inspired with Good and we experience joy and entertainment.

We need not judge joy or quantify it. We do not need to measure the quantity of joy in ourselves or others. We do not create or distribute joy. Joy is as constant as our Good is. Joy is everlasting and in all things. All of our entertainment is for our enjoyment. All of our experience in this realm likewise is for our enjoyment and entertainment.

We find our joy through various and infinite means. Our Good is consistent therefore our joy is as well.

We cannot be arrogant or judgmental because we are no more or less Good than our Good. And all that we have and experience in our Good is divinely perfect. Delay of joy is needless. We abide in our Good. We look and see with love and joy.

We are certain in our Good. In our Good, we are not capable of suspiciousness or viciousness. In Good, we cannot experience shifting perceptions. We are never in conflict nor do we have conflicting views. We never forget that we are Good. We always see lovingly. We experience eternal happiness.

There is never a time when we are inadequate nor can we ever feel inadequate. We do not have to try to escape from a sense of inadequacy for we are perfect and are abundantly provided for. We are happy and joyous in all of our fantasy and entertainment. Words such as judgement, discernment, and evaluation are all the same and have absolutely no purpose in our Good for we are sufficient, whole and always adequate.

***

My apologies for where I have interjected some personal conclusions into the text. Denials and affirmations are a technique that apply the emotions to do the thinking rather than the intellect. So at any point in reading my translations you did not feel comfortable, then it would be best to re-write the material to better suit your emotions. I did not continue with the rest of the Chapters of the ACIM text, but to do so would provide you great insight as to many of the spiritual principles the book is supposed to provide.

However, during editing, I did extract one of my personal insertions and decided rather to include it with my comments:

Individual thought does not:
- have meaning;
- have value;
- solve problems;
- bring rewards;
- keep one occupied and feeling useful;
- plan or achieve successful goals;
- protect and support survival;

- bring happiness.

Spiritual thought does:
- have meaning;
- have value;
- solve problems;
- bring rewards;
- keep one occupied and feeling useful;
- plan or achieve successful goals;
- protect and support survival;
- bring happiness.

Chapter 3 : This realm of time, space and matter

So another snag that I ran into in creating this book, is how to deal with the misperceived negative aspect of this present world of time, space and matter. My solution has been derived from Yogananda's concept which is that we are here in this realm of time, space and matter to be entertained. I am supposing that in eternity, some may wish to experience an imagined lack of Good for a relatively short duration in the realm of time, space and matter for entertainment. So I attempted to resolve this dilemma with the following:

We are always free to experience unreality or lack and we can readily return to our Good whenever we tire of such an experience. Our knowledge is always total so we can experience littleness only for temporary entertainment for we could never permanently deny our knowledge of our Good. All that we could choose outside our Good for entertainment will never fulfill us to the complete fullness that our Good provides. Our Good is inclusive and complete whereas what we choose for entertainment will be exclusive and limited.

We can even choose to experience an ego, but to do so could never have any effect upon our permanent Good. There is never anything that can arise from our forms of entertainment that can take on any real meaning. Our Good allows us to entertain the meaningless without any ill consequence.

Our Good is complete and in our Good, so are we. We can entertain questions and evaluate data ad infinitum without ever affecting our Good. We are free to listen to an ego without ever disrupting Good. Listening to an ego can do no harm to our Good nor can it ever upset anyone unless they choose to be upset for their own entertainment. We never need to make any terms with our Good for our Good is all encompassing, approving and supporting. We have everything from our Good and our Good does not need us to offer our Good anything.

Our Good, being the ultimate and all-encompassing, requires no comparison description. Descriptive words such as magnificent, grand or majestic are unnecessary because they would indicate that there are degrees of our Good; and forms of lesser Good cannot exist. All forms of any entertainment we choose, to include the ego as well, cannot be compared to our Good for our entertainment is purely benign and meaningless fantasy.

Our Good provides us freedom of choice without any negative or meaningless repercussions or punishment. With our complete knowledge of Good intrinsic in our being that can never be forgotten, our choices of entertainment can never harm us nor deprive us from our Good. We can neither inflate or deflate our Good, but we can be entertained by the fantasy of such ridiculousness.

Enemies and foes are for entertainment purposes only and cannot exist in our Good. We are free to imagine departure or separation from our Good without ever incurring any real damage or corollary. We are free to experience grandiosity or despair but we will always return to our Good whenever we tire of the experience. We always know that an experience of less, lack or littleness is for entertainment in eternity but our fantasies for fun can never be real.

We can war, attack or crucify in our fantasies without ever affecting our constant Good. We are free to imagine leaving our Good or returning to our Good ad infinitum without ever changing the reality of our Good.

Delusions are for entertainment as well, but in our True reality we need not undo anything. We can entertain self-abasement and then seek relief just for the experience of occupying time. We can enter and leave the entertainment realm of time, matter and space as often as we wish. None of our fantasy creations can exceed or fall short of our constant Good.

Ego can influence or not. Ego can be threatened or not. Ego can experience all things in the realm of time, space and matter, but ego is not our Good. We do not need to be threatened by ego, but we are always free to choose that experience for as long as we desire.

Our Good created ego with everything else, so our ego is a part of all that is Good. However, ego is not omniscient, omnipotent, constant, infinite or eternal. We do not need to despise ego but we are free to do so if we choose. Ego is just for our entertainment in this realm of time, space and matter. We are free to choose to be sinners or saints in this realm of entertainment and our Good will oversee our safety. Such as movies, TV show and video games, an amusement park is another metaphor for what we presently and temporarily experience in this world of time, space, energy and matter.

Although we are invulnerable, we can choose to experience vulnerability. Although we have no use for grandiosity or humility, we can single these out of our great Good for our entertainment just as we can choose which programs we desire to watch or which games we choose to play. We are always returned to our Good by Good's unconditional loving kindness and infinite grace. Our temporal existence guarantees our joyous return. Our permanent grandeur cannot be altered or destroyed and nothing from this realm of entertainment can affect our grandeur. We always exist in our Good no matter what illusional experience we may choose in this realm.

We can pretend to have no knowledge of our Good in this realm just for the experience without ever having any effect upon our true reality. And we are free to ride the roller coaster over and over to our hearts desire even though during the ride we were frightened. No dreadful consequence could ever harm us or keep us from our Good.

Good is abundant, unlimited and endless and we are blessed with unlimited, endless and abundant Good. We are always in the mind of our Good and cannot forget it, abuse it or lose it. Despair, littleness and grandiosity are for entertainment purposes only and have no real effect upon us or our Good in eternity. Our Good allows us to experience extremes, inconsistencies and frequent change for temporary entertainment because we exist in the infinite and eternal realm of Good. And it is all Good.

Our Good does not vacillate but we are free to vacillate just for the experience. Experience cannot affect our permanent knowledge of our Good. The experience of delusion, illusion and deception are for our entertainment, but do not add or subtract one iota from our Good. We can choose to temporarily experience insanity, sanity or both in various degrees. We can be depressed or exalted or bipolar, but we can never deny Good. In this realm of time, space, matter and energy, we are free to be selective, prejudicial, arrogant, proud or alone without any influence upon our reality in Good. Nothing could ever deprive us from our Good and our Good cannot deprive us of anything we desire to experience.

There are no substitutes for our Good nor can our Good be replaced. We are never missing and therefore we need not return anywhere. Our value is constant and magnificent. We can only be as we always have been which is Good. We have no reason or desire to degrade or devalue ourselves or our Good. Good is invulnerable. We never need to ask for anything because we have already received everything and nothing we wish will be denied nor could anything we do ever cause any real harm to ourselves as a whole.

With the above being said, our Good loves us so much, that at any point in the eternal and infinite now we desire to experience a realm where there is no Good, we can temporarily do so do our hearts desire. We can experience a realm of self-centeredness, a world of lack, a place without love, etc. We can experience the pain of greed, the suffering of lack, rage, violence, treachery, and so on, just like in the movies and TV. And just like movies and TV, there are no permanent consequences. And just like movies and TV, you can come and go as you please.

In our eternal and infinite Good, there is such a thing as "free will" where we are free to experience ignorance or nothing. Although we cannot permanently deny our Good and permanently live in isolation and have nothing, we are always allowed the temporary experience. We are free to experience dissatisfaction, but our Good will always maintain our permanent happiness.

Our will is committed to our Good, but we are always free to temporarily experience the opposite of our Good because have been and will always be free in our Good. We have "free will" to experience whatever we choose pro tem with impunity. Our Good will never abandon us no matter what our choice might be.

We can choose to have trouble with personal relationships. We can believe that we are unable to control our emotions. We can pretend to fall prey to misery and depression or be unable to enjoy life. We can imagine being full of fear, being useless or unhappy. But now that we understand the technique of "Denial and Affirmation" we can readily return to our Good in the present.

There can be only one explanation for the experience of anything contradictory to perfection everywhere, now; and that is that we requested something else to experience. In an eternity of perfection, we may have asked to experience something that is not perfection and subsequently we were given what we requested.

But there can be no harm in our experience, no more than what we might receive by watching a movie. If we watch a frightening movie, we are frightened. But we can always leave the theater and return home whenever we like. The movie is no more the truth than any experience away from our Good. We can be entertained but we cannot be deprived of our Good.

Our Good is merciful and wills only our complete happiness. There is no way we could ever disobey our Good. So if we choose to be frightened for the experience, no harm could ever come our way from such event. Laws for Good are all encompassing therefore there can be no bad. Our temporary exemption from peace is only for our entertainment. But we will always return home safe and sound.

Our Good will never deny us any diversion that we request nor will our Good ever allow any harm to come to us from such amusement in our eternal existence. We can imagine denying ourselves everything to pursue distraction from eternity but then we can always return for rest and reprieve. The illusion of isolation, loneliness and fear are only for our leisure.

We can experience darkness at will, but there is no need to dispel darkness because darkness cannot be real in a realm of all-encompassing light. We are free to feel hopelessness but there is no need to reject it because there is only love in our reality. This world does not need peace. This world is not real. This life experience is not real and we can choose to have our present experience change back to the Truth whenever we grow tired of the frightening movie.

There is no need for love in this pretend world of illusion for we can always stop our loveless experience and return to our Good. And we are free to go back and forth as much as we can stand. Our Good only chooses our happiness, safety and protection from harm.

In equality we need not a leader to follow. In our Good, we never need salvation. Being forever Good we have no need for healing. There is no possible way to ever separate us from our Good. We are unequivocally united in our Good. We are equally powerful as we are equally Good.

Whether we choose to temporarily experience pain or joy, we are still Good and we need not be saved from any experience. We choose our temporary conditions knowing that no harm will ever come our way. Even if we choose to temporarily forget our Good, our Good could never abandon us nor leave us in harm's way. We will always return to our true reality which is Good.

Our reality is changeless and complete peace and joy, yet we can be entertained with the imaginings of the impossible. With entertainment, there is no foul or any harm because we can never be harmed. But we can imagine what it would be like. This can be the only explanation for the life experience upon earth. Earth must be one of many sophisticated playgrounds for the immortal.

Our holy union in our Good can never be overcome, but we are always free to imagine separation and individuality. We are always free to experience sorrow or separation, but it is never permanent. Our mind can determine whatever condition we wish yet eventually as we tire from the experience of weakness we return to our Good. We cannot be denied of whatever we choose, but we can choose again and again. Our imagining, whether we separate or join, can have no effect upon our Good or Truth.

Good would never oppose our decision to not experience our Good, but our Good will always be there for our return when we change our mind. Our perfect equality cannot be realized through domination. Perfect Love cannot oppose us, yet perfect Love will always support us. We will always be free, but we will never have the power to denigrate Good one iota. We will always be enveloped in Love and Good no matter what our imaginings may be.

There are an infinite number of representatives of Good to bail us out whenever our imaginings are no longer wanted. We are given freedom but we are also provided protection and safety. Because "all there is" is Good no harm could ever touch us in our exercise of freedom. No limits have been set upon us. There are no laws to break or disobey. We are perfectly safe. Any imaginings we choose outside our Good can only be temporary and our rescue is immediate upon our request.

Disassociation and delusion are allowable choices for entertainment. There is no choice we could ever make that would ever harm our Good or ourselves. We can temporarily block our knowledge of Good just to experience what that might be like, but our knowledge of Good can never be permanently removed. And when we no longer enjoy the experience of being without, there are many qualified and competent entities of Good overlooking our experience of individuality waiting to adjust our experience for the better or to bring us back into our perfection.

We are allowed to experience individuality, self-sufficiency or helplessness without ever any real danger or harm because the experience is only temporary and unreal. Our Good would never deny us any temporary and unreal experience we so choose for whatever reason. In our Good there is never any real danger. The power of our Good is far beyond any real danger and our Good never actually leaves us in any temporary or unreal experience we may choose. Our Good is always invincible and undivided.

We never actually leave the whole in our experience of being a separate entity. We can never un-unite or secede permanently, but our Good never denies us our entertainment and imaginings.
Our present worldly experience is neither evil nor wrong. Our temporary blindness from our Good is for entertainment purposes only. We cannot behold this world and loose our Good.

Our temporary illusions do not replace our Good. This world is for entertainment; enjoy the ride or not. Nothing in this world, no action, thought or emotion in this world can take away our eternal Good. This worldly experience can neither add nor subtract from our Good. No matter what decisions we make or actions we take in the imaginary realm of time and space, when we tire of the experience we are always welcomed home like the prodigal son.

In this realm of experience we presently find ourselves, we experience very small portions of the eternal and infinite by imagining happenings in periods of linear time and locations within three dimensional space. We use very limited language and intellect to perceive and communicate. Our experience cannot harm us nor can it increase our status one iota.

In this world, we imagine the impossibility of a hierarchy just for its entertainment value. Our life here allows us to be entertained with the impossibility of duality. We use thoughts, emotions, language and action to appreciate the entertainment. Everything that we think, feel, communicate or do is only for our entertainment and we are thoroughly entertained constantly by thought, emotion, communication and action during our temporary stay.

We can imagine limitation and imagine a need to accept more or imagine that there are those with less. We can imagine duality, separation, limitation and death. We can imagine degrees, divisions and categories. We are allowed to take temporary excursions into our imaginings and be entertained by the process. But we cannot create because there is nothing left to create.

Our will is always for Good. There is nothing else to will. To be entertained by experiencing anything and everything for eternity is our will. We can even choose to temporarily experience nothing. Yet our will is always in accordance with our Good. There is no other real alternative.

We are always free to imagine the unreal. This is not contradiction or hypocrisy because our freedom to choose is Good. No harm or foul can ever occur from our choices because we are infinitely and eternally Good. And there is only Good and nothing other than Good.

We can imagine forgiving others for the fun of it, but they are never in need of our forgiveness either.

In our Good, we are aware that there is neither a father nor a son. In unconditional love and equality there is nothing that needs to be glorified, worshipped or obeyed. We do not have to align our will with some other entity. In our Good we cannot be apart but we are always free to imagine being a part rather than the whole. We are allowed to imagine living in a lie rather than the Truth with absolutely no ill consequence in our reality. If we so choose our Good allows us to be alone.

Our Good is all knowledgeable and can never be ignorant. Our Good is aware of every decision and choice we make and provides us unconditional love for doing so. We are never in need of forgiveness.

We are and have always been awake to the knowledge of our Good. No reawakening or journey is required. Only the Truth of our Good exists, but we are free to experience anything we so desire without harm to ourselves or our imaginary fellows. There is no real goal that needs to be achieved in our imaginary experiences. The objective of each of our infinite experiences is just that we are entertained.

Attack or defense in this imaginary physical realm can cause no actual harm. We can equate ourselves to a physical body for entertainment purposes but there never shall be any consequences from this experience. We are free to experience egotism or depression in the imagination with no harm. We can experience judging others or being judged. The human experience like all other experience is only temporary and has no effect upon our Good or our true reality.

This imaginary world that provides us entertainment does not need healing nor does anyone within the experience require our help.

There is no action that we must take in order to salvage our Good. Good cannot be hurt, harmed or altered.

The body can be harmed, hurt or destroyed but whatever takes place will have no real effect upon us. We can choose to imagine being more powerful or powerless just for the thrill of it, but our Good can only stand fast within its perfection and never be affected by our imaginings. When we bore of any particular form of imaginary and temporary entertainment we simply revert back to our Good to enjoy our Good as long as we desire.

There is no right or wrong; there is just Good. We can neither attack or be attacked in our true reality of Good. Everything else is just for our entertainment in eternity. We are free to do as we please without ever any chance of doing harm to our real selves or others. We are free to hate, to murder, to love, to be loved for nothing in this imagined entertainment center is real. And when we so desire, we return to our Good without judgement or punishment. There is only reward for each and every one in our Good. There are no select few or chosen ones for there is no hierarchy in equality.

We can imagine experiencing loss, depression, demoralization, defiance and the like with impunity. And we are free to change whatever course we have set to another at any given time within this life experience. We are free to reject one experience and then choose another. We are free to love, forgive, care, and enjoy as well. We are free to mix and match and choose an infinity of combinations. We are free to be good in one area of our experience and bad in another area of our experience.

Our true power can never be lost or denied. We are always connected to our Good. Our communication with Good is constant and continuous. In eternity, there is no creation or a creator. We are all, always have been and will always be. We can ask ourselves, "Either there is an eternity or not; either there is an infinity or there is not?" If the answer is "yes" then it is obvious that there can be no beginning or no end; and everything already exists. However we are free to choose exactly how much of eternity and infinity we wish to experience in our imaginary time and space. And we are also free to choose the answer as "No" or make up some combination that we wish to experiment with for our entertainment. We can never be wrong in our Good.

Fantasy is Good. We can experience fantasy only as Good because our imagination is used only for our Good. The impossible cannot be imagined or actualized. Only reality exists. Although reality cannot be found in fantasy, fantasy does provide entertainment.

The history of the planet cannot be real or true for it is for entertainment only. Our experience here is pure fantasy for entertainment purposes only. We have the ability to choose our fantasies and entertainment with impunity. Nightmares are optional for entertainment but have no effect upon our ultimate Good. But no one can teach condemnation or advocate fear. We need not fear retribution nor retaliation because we all are always in our Good.

We cannot hold on to an insane belief but we can be entertained by the fantasy of one without any harm or damage to our Good. For our Good is invincible yet allowing, tolerant and approving. No matter what form of entertainment we choose to temporarily experience, our core, which is Good, always remains constant and omnipotent. The grandeur of our Good is constant and endless, but we can choose to be little and lament for the experience and entertainment without ever the chance of actually losing or being separated by our Good.

Peace is an attribute of Good and cannot be found in this physical world. To look for peace in the external only leads us to mental illness, despair and delusion. It is only by placing Good in our heart and our mind that the external conditions we experience change for the better.

Likewise, Love is a concept that the conscious mind cannot comprehend because Love exists in the Superconscious Mind. Only Good can correct the seeming conditions of lack of Love. Alone, without Good, our conscious mind has insufficient power to improve our perception of the external conditions of this world. To improve our perception of external conditions, we must unite with our Good.

***

In Dante's "Inferno" the sign above the gateway to Hell reads, "All Ye who enter, abandon all hope", but what those imaginary figures in an imaginary Hell did not understand is that as soon as they are willing to abandon all hope they will be released from their imaginary Hell. In Dante's poem, the fictional Satan is continuously flapping his wings to escape the ice his feet are trapped into, but if he were to stop flapping his wings, the ice would melt. Dante's sign is actually the answer to their dilemma.

Likewise with us. As soon as we are willing to stop calling the lie the Truth and the Truth a lie, then we too shall be released from our temporary and imaginary Hell.

Chapter 4 : Miracles and Actions for Good

With the technique of "Denial and Affirmation", one can take the lie and convert it into the Truth. Changing a negative perception, thought, emotion or behavior into a positive one is this book's definition of a miracle. By using this technique, we perform many miracles in this realm by changing our consciousness from the negative to the positive. And as we do this, so do we receive our Good.

So, with that being said, I have translated some of the ACIM definitions of a miracle into definitions of "Good" and "Actions for Good". We need not do anything, but somehow we think we might be bored with that, so most of us want to do something that provides desirable consequences. So read my version of some of the ACIM definitions and see if you don't get some ideas as to what action you should take to keep yourself positively entertained:

1. Good is everywhere, eternal and infinite. Good cannot be compromised.
2. We come from Good as expressions of Good. We are an expression of maximum Good.
3. We are always connected to a source of Good far beyond human calculation and intelligence.
4. We are channels for Good; we are vehicles for the expression of Good.
5. Our actions for Good come from Good.
6. Our actions for Good are easy and effortless.
7. In order to genuinely perform acts of Good, miracles might be necessary.
8. Miracles can be defined as the shifting our attachment from lower order material consciousness to a higher order of Good (Spiritual) consciousness. Miracles can be accomplished with denials, affirmations, meditation and prayer.

9. Through actions for Good, those who seem to have more Love can supply the seeming lack of Love to those who seem to have less. This is most often accomplished by denying the negative perception and affirming our Good through meditation and prayer and sending Truth and Love to those who seem to have less.

10. Regular and consistent denial, affirmation, meditation, prayer and actions for Good create a Spiritually awake state of mind where incorrect thinking, motives, emotions or behavior no longer exist.

11. A Spiritually awake mind is a sane mind that affirms only Truth and denies all else.

12. There are no degrees of magnitude or order of difficulty for actions for Good, therefore actions for Good should make no distinction among degrees of misperception. Actions for Good are to correct perception regardless of the degree or type of error.

13. Actions for Good supply both the giver and the receiver with Good.

14. There are no limits to Good. Through our expression and sharing of Good, more Good is received.

15. Communication with Good is conducted primarily through denial, affirmation, meditation, prayer and channeling of Good through our thoughts, words, emotions and actions.

16. Our thoughts can represent higher order (spiritual) or lower order (material) reality. Consistent denial and affirmation with Good is necessary to maintain the higher order of thought in our consciousness which, in turn, creates our improved experiential reality.

17. Our actions for Good and of Love are not of our own making. Our actions for Good come from communication with our Good. Consciously selected actions for Good can be misguided by our ego.

18. Actions for Good do not necessarily require physical action. Our Good comes to us through our denial, affirmations, meditation and prayer.

19. Actions for Good are not to be used as spectacles to induce belief or approval. They are not actions for Good, if the motive behind them is wrong or misunderstood.
20. Actions for Good undo our focus of the past or future.
21. Actions for Good instill the Good which is the basis of our True Reality.
22.. Actions for Good bear witness to the Truth. Actions for Good unite our minds into the Truth.
23. In this world of duality, there can be creative use of the mind or uncreative (destructive) use of the mind. Actions for Good are the way out of the world of duality and are the path back to the Spiritual world of Truth.
24. Good is based upon laws of infinity and eternity; Good supersedes all alleged laws of matter, space or time.
25. Time, space and matter is provided to learn how to consistently perform Actions for Good. Once we have acquired habitual Good, time, space and matter will no longer be necessary.
26. Only eternity and infinity are real. We use the illusion of time, space and matter constructively to seek and find only Good. No effort is wasted. As we learn and teach Good, limitless Good avails Itself toward our progression.
27. Actions for Good increase the supply of Good for the giver as well as the receiver.
28. Actions for Good heal in the sense that they shift our mind away from the sense of low order reality to a higher order of Good reality.
29. Actions for Good allow us to recognize our own as well as our neighbor's inestimable worth simultaneously.
30. Actions for Good reawaken our awareness of Spirit, showing us that the material is not the Truth.
31. As we extend love, forgiveness, mercy and kindness to others, our Good supplies us with an infinite source of the same.
32. Only Good exists. All else is deception. Deception can be brought out from hiding and dispelled through actions for Good.

33. We often call deception fear and the removal of fear as healing. Healing is the correction of our perspective so that we see and experience only Good.

34. Good can change our mind for the better. Good can abolish sickness and death. Good can eradicate hatred, bias, segregation and war.

35. Actions for Good eliminate all delusions of this material world and will return us to the image of Good in our consciousness and our experience.

36. Good will lovingly come to help us, whenever we ask.

37. Sin is only error in our thinking and incorrect perception of what is the Truth.

38. Only in duality can the displeasure of sin be experienced. Sin does not exist in the Realm of Good.

39. Focusing on sin and frightening ourselves is very painful.

40. As Good assists us in undoing error we become free from fear. Instead of focusing our consciousness on the lack of Good, we put our awareness into the hands of Good, and with Good's help we return to the realm of Good. As Good is restored to our awareness, we learn to listen to more Good, learn more Good and do more Good. The rich get richer.

41. We must be willing and ready to perform actions for Good. Performing actions for Good will bring belief and repeated actions for Good will bring faith. Faith will bring confidence, poise, peace and calm.

42. Our increasing and progressive expression of Good will achieve Good's purpose which is to restore everyone to their right mind, sanity.

43. Again performing Actions for Good does not necessarily require physical action. Physical action is in the realm of the physical and often is misunderstood, misconstrued and unbeneficial for the giver or receiver.

44 The superconscious mind contains knowledge of all that is Good. The subconscious mind creates the action of the conscious mind. Both the subconscious and the superconscious mind can be

contacted with meditation and prayer. Correct methods of meditation and then prayer remove the conscious ego mind from the equation and allows the knowledge of correct thinking of the superconscious to be placed into the subconscious mind. The conscious mind then performs actions for Good by default from what is stored into the subconscious, but the conscious mind must allow this and willingly take action of routine meditation and prayer to make this happen.

45. "I am" is always in Ego, which cannot be part of our Good.

46. In order to join as souls, correction of our conscious and subconscious mind is necessary. We do this joined in denial, affirmation, meditation and pray.

47. We must return from insanity and move on toward Good.

48. We cannot return to sanity without the help from our Good.

49. Joined as souls, we are Spirit.

50. We always return to our Good.

Appendix 1 – Meditation – Inner Sensitivity - Teaching of the Inner Christ

Meditation is an altered state of consciousness. There are methods of meditation established that when followed allow us to release our normal waking state of consciousness, release our past troubles, release our worries about the future, our emotional disturbances and enter a place of peace and quiet. It is like a small vacation for the brain and body systems and just as rejuvenating as eight hours of sleep. Meditation provides the same feelings you get sitting by a mountain lake or walking through a forest or laying in the sun in a quiet cove by the beach. And after meditation you feel recharged and in a better state of mind than when you began.

Hypnosis also has the same effect as meditation, but hypnosis is designed to contact your subconscious mind. The purpose of meditation is to contact your higher self, a loving, all knowing side of yourself that can provide you answers and can answer prayer. Some call it superconscious mind; some call it the Inner Christ; I call it Good. There are many other names as well found in many other spiritual teachings. Look for the similarities rather than the differences and you will be greatly rewarded.

Also in the meditative trance-like state, some have visual experiences; some auditory or a feeling nature; so allow yourself freedom to experiment and explore. There are many wonderful books, recordings and videos for meditation. Personally I took classes and found group meditation to be very powerful. I also met a wonderful quality of people to associate with.

An organization known as The Teaching of the Inner Christ provides information on meditation in their book entitled BEING A CHRIST - Inner Sensitivity (Intuitional) Training Course by Ann P. Meyer and Peter V. Meyer. The following is liberally transcribed from that book to provide the reader information on meditation (the editor recommends that the reader of this proposal read their text or take their courses in order to gain the specific information provided by their teaching and in order to gain a fuller experience with your Good): *"In this Teaching we define deep meditation as an awareness trance, in order to emphasize the fact that we are very much aware in the state of deep meditation. To an observer, a person sitting motionless in a deep meditation may appear to have lost conscious awareness, but they are actually keenly aware and very conscious of the inner levels of their Being, while oblivious to their outer environment. The word trance comes from the word transcend, which means go beyond. The prefix "trans" means to go across. This suggests a movement in consciousness. Awareness Trance is a movement in consciousness to the inner Good, taking awareness with us. When we are in an awareness trance we are not asleep or dreaming, but are alert, in an altered consciousness, at a deeper level of mind, a level which we are normally unconscious. The awareness trance or deep meditation is a state of relaxation and concentration -- that is relaxation of the outer levels of consciousness and concentration on the deep inner levels. During meditation the subconscious mind is not listening to the voice of another individual, nor to the voice of one's own outer self, but to the voice of Spirit inside. Deep meditation is absolute, undivided, concentration upon the Inner Self. The practice of deep meditation is perfectly natural, as well as extremely beneficial. We are primarily intuitive beings, designed to draw forth from our inner resources of wisdom all the knowledge required for us to fulfill the needs of our lives. The flow of intuitive knowledge from deep within our minds would be constant and all sufficient if human beings had not for the most part, turned their attention outward upon the physical world, with the resulting loss of daily awareness of their Inner Good. To pause to listen to the Inner Good, to listen completely and intently, is the most natural and helpful practice a human being can engage in. In mind there is no matter, space or time. All action of mind takes place anywhere and everywhere. "The Kingdom of Heaven is within you".*

The first step of this type of meditation is to remove all attention from our outer environment (where our attention is focused most of the time) by becoming still, closing the eyes (seeing, hearing, smelling and other senses) and being willing to let the world go by for a while. The second step is to remove attention from our physical body. (We do this by employing complete body relaxation methods as discussed in the TIC text.) Having relaxed all awareness of both the environment and the physical body, it is now possible to take the attention to the next level inward, the conscious mind (the intellect). By now we may begin to have the feeling that we are merely a mental being; we may have forgotten temporarily that we have a physical body. This level of trance, which may be called light-meditation is quite usual; many people reach it while deep in thought (or deep into the present work task in front of them). The next step of our journey inward is the relaxation of the intellect (the reasoning mind) which allows the attention to be drawn still deeper, to the subconscious mind. Now we are aware only of feelings, deep memories, or visualizations. This is the subliminal state, which you have experienced many times while drifting off to sleep or awakening. The difference here is that we are in conscious control and are able to maintain awareness on the subliminal level without going to sleep. We are awake and alert with deeply relaxed bodies. Next we relax the subconscious mind and thus are able to transfer awareness to the inmost level of Spirit (the super conscious, the Christ Self, the I AM, the Good, etc.). At this time there may be a temporary feeling of upheaval as we cross for the first time the psychic barrier composed of long-held beliefs in separation from the Inner Self. Going through it can cause a great vibrational change in the physical and mental bodies" (a spiritual experience or awakening, a psychic change, etc.) *"As we approach the inner levels of our being by rendering ourselves completely relaxed and receptive, the Good often takes the opportunity to reach out for us and draw us inward, through this mental barrier. The sudden vibration change may cause us to tremble, shake, weep, laugh",* (see a bright light, etc.) *as the case may be. After we have penetrated to the innermost levels, we feel a great sense of release and peace. At this level we are aware only of Good thoughts - Truth, Goodness, Love, Peace, Harmony, and Oneness with life. Spirit gives no recognition to the error thinking of the outer mind, or to the collective race mind consciousness. The Soul within is our true identity. Having reached the depths of our being, through the process of relaxation and concentration, we now can feed upon the wisdom, love, life and power of the Universal Good. We receive new truths, new solutions to our problems, and we are submerged into creative thought. From this inner reservoir many people receive healing, spiritual power and a replenishing of the life substance of mind and body." If we are eternal, then we have many more dimensions to experience, but with the knowledge of prayer and meditation we have a choice as to which direction and what quality of experience we wish to have in this and the next experience.*

The TIC text goes on to describe the wonderful benefits of meditation: "A deep meditation, whether short or long, results in a lifting of consciousness for any person who goes into it with this intent. As you go deep within yourself there is a temporary merging of the outer levels of your mind (which are often influenced by error thinking) with the pure inner mind, which knows only reality - perfection now. Each time you lift your consciousness through meditation, you achieve a permanent change in your beliefs and attitudes. You become more like your true inner Good. As you learn to engage in deep meditation regularly, you will experience an entirely new way of viewing life, enjoying high ideals and ideas, harmonious thinking and living, peace of mind and physical health. The benefits of deep bodily relaxation are in themselves most important, for many people today are not able to completely relax the body, even in sleep. Improved relaxation results in better health, balance of living, poise, and sense of wellbeing, agility, flexibility, and a prosperous life. The relaxed body is vibrating on a higher frequency and more attuned to the inner Good, and thus more able to be fed by the universal energy (prana). The relaxed person is more receptive to Truth and better able to enjoy living. A deep meditation furnishes a temporary relief or refreshment from the sea of race-mind error thinking (a.k.a. Ego) in which we live in daily. Although each of us is an individual center of awareness, we are in the one mind, and the error beliefs of fear, lack, illness, disharmony, etc. which exist in the composite memory of the human race often influence our individual minds. We achieve dominion over these error beliefs by making regular visits into pure, fresh consciousness of the Inner Good Mind. Practicing meditation on a regular basis also deepens the life expression. We become less emotionally embroiled in our problems and the trouble of others; we become more objective, thus achieving command over them. The outer personality keeps in closer touch with the Inner Good, allowing the outward flow of Love and Good which feeds the mind and the feeling nature and the body. False personality facades disintegrate and the real person begins to express at last. Those who meditate regularly are aware of many sensations of power feeding, spiritual quickening, surges of energy,--and they actually begin to require less and lighter foods to maintain bodily health and vigor. The physical body functions more efficiently and becomes more youthful, lighter, more beautiful and more like the perfect Good."

The Teachings of Inner Christ organization and many other such Spiritual Organizations have much more quality information on prayer and meditation and spiritual development for those interested.

Appendix 2 – Meditation – Self Realization Fellowship – Paramahansa Yogananda

The Self-Realization Fellowship founded in the U.S. in 1920 by Paramahansa Yogananda also provides some excellent information on meditation, however the information must be obtained from their office (for a nominal fee) and it is requested not to disperse their information (probably because of editors such as myself, who only take the portions they see fit and pass on diluted or misconstrued information). The following information which is available comes from Yogananda's commentary of The Bhagavad Gita. I extract some of the written information for the benefit of the reader and to perhaps introduce them to further investigation of the Self-Realization Fellowship.

"By the special technique of Kriya Yoga, the ingoing breath of prana and the outgoing breath of apana are converted into cool and warm currents. In the beginning of the practice of Kriya Yoga, the devotee feels the cool prana current going up the spine and the warm apana current going down the spine, in accompaniment with the ingoing and outgoing breath. The advanced Kriya Yogi finds that the inhaling breath of prana and the exhaling breath of apana have been evened, neutralized or extinguished; he feels only the cool current of prana going up through the spine and the warm current of apana going down through the spine"..."In successful meditation, the Kriya Yogi converts the two distinct impulses of inhalation and exhalation into two life currents, the cool prana and the warm apana, felt in the spine. He then realizes the truth of Jesus' saying -- that a man is not required to depend on external breath (or on "bread" or any other outward sustenance) as a condition of bodily existence. The yogi perceives the cool and warm currents in the spine to be constantly and magnetically pulling an extra voltage of current from the omnipresent cosmic life force ever flowing through the medulla. He gradually finds that these two spinal currents become converted into one life force, magnetically drawing reinforcements of prana from all the bodily

cells and nerves. This strengthened life current flows upward to the point between the eyebrows and is seen as the tricolored spherical astral eye: a luminous sun, in the center of which is a blue sphere encircling a bright scintillating star. Jesus referred to this single eye in the center of the forehead and to the truth that the body is essentially formed of light, in the following words: "If therefore thine eye be single, thy whole body shall be full of light..." "By practice of Kriya, the yogi scientifically detaches his mind from gross sensory perceptions and realized that consciousness and life force (prana or cosmic light) are the basis of all matter. The Kriya Yogi adopts a scientific method to divert his mind and reason from his perception of physical flesh; he perceives the body as light and consciousness by rising above the gross perception of breath. All inner experiences like that of subconscious sleep can only take place when the consciousness of breath disappears. The Kriya Yogi has no need or desire to withhold breath forcibly in the lungs; he becomes mentally so calm that he feels himself to be aloof of breath. By the practice of Kriya Yoga he can consciously and at will attain the breathless state and sustain life in his body solely by the cool and warm currents flowing through the spine and trickling down from the spiritual eye"..."When the devotee is convinced by Kriya Yoga that he can live solely by the inner source of cosmic energy, he realized that the body is a wave of the all-sufficing cosmic ocean of life. By the special technique of Kriya Yoga, the devotee--through perfect calmness, though a greater supply of energy distilled from oxygen in the Kriya breath, and through enhanced flow of cosmic energy coming into the body through the medulla-is less and less subject to the necessity for breathing. By deeper Kriya Yoga the bodily life, ordinarily dependent on reinforcement by life force distilled from gross outer sources, begins to be sustained by the cosmic life only: then breathing (inhalation and exhalation) ceases. All the trillions of bodily cells become like regenerating dry batteries needing nothing but the inner "electricity" recharged from the cosmic source of life. In this way the bodily cells remain in a suspended state -- that is, they neither grow or decay. They are sustained and vitalized directly from the life-energy dynamos in the brain and spine. When the cells cease to grow, they are not required to depend on the life current distilled from oxygen, sunshine, solids and liquids but on the inner source of cosmic life. Kriya Yoga pranayama withdraws life force from the activities unnecessary--and unites that bodily prana with the cosmic life force; man's slavish dependence on breath is thus realized to be delusory. When the yogi expert in pranayama can thus disengage at will the life force from its bondage of oxygen and so on, he can immortalize it by uniting with Cosmic Life"... "The prana and apana currents flowing in the spine become calm and even, generating a tremendous magnetic power and joy. As meditation deepens, the downward-flowing apana current and the upward flowing prana current become neutralized into one ascending current, seeking its source in the cerebrum. Breath is still, life is still, sensations and thoughts are dissolved. The divine light of life and consciousness perceived by the devotee in the cerebrospinal centers becomes one with the Cosmic Light and Cosmic Consciousness. Acquisition of the power of this realization enables the yogi to consciously detach his soul from identification with the body. He becomes free from the distressing bondage of desires (the body's attachment and longing for sensory gratification), fears (the thought of possible nonfulfillment of desires), and anger (the emotional response to obstacles that thwart fulfillment of desires). These three impelling forces in man are the greatest enemies of soul bliss; they must be destroyed by that devotee who aspires to reach God. Life force is the connecting--and disconnecting--link between matter and Spirit, between body consciousness and soul consciousness. The ordinary man does not know how to get at the bodily prana directly. Therefore, this life force works automatically to enliven the body and senses and by the medium of breath ties man's attention solely to his physical existence. But by the use of Kriya Yoga the devotee learns how to distill life force out of breath and how to control prana. With this control, the life force can be switched off at will from the five sense channels and turned inward, thus diverting the soul's attention from the perception of material phenomena to the perception of Spirit. By the scientific step by step method, the yogi ascends from the senses in actuality and not by a mere ineffectual mental diversion from them. He completely disconnects mind and reason and attention from the body, by switching off the life force from the five senses. He learns scientifically to divert to the spine and brain the currents from his five sense channels and thus unite his consciousness with the joy of higher spiritual perceptions in the seven centers" (Chakras). "When he is able to remain immersed in divine bliss even in his active state, he does not become further involved in desires to enjoy external objects. Radiating the calmness of divine realizations, he is not disturbed by the springing up of fear and anger from non-fulfillments of material desires. He finds his soul no longer tied to matter but forever united to the cosmic bliss of Spirit."..."Methods of spiritual freedom are various, but the actual attainment of liberation by ascent through the spine is universal. Whether through: (1) Bhakta - intense devotion and prayer, (2) Jnani - pure discrimination, (3) Karma Yoga - nonattached selfless actions, or (4) Kriya Yoga; the consciousness purified and concentrated thereby still makes its final ascent to God through the subtle spinal channels through which it descended into flesh. The principle of Kriya Yoga therefore is not a formula of a sectarian rite, but a science through the application of which the individual may realize how his soul descended into the body and became identified with the senses and reunited with Spirit by a scientific method of meditation. This route of descent and ascension is the one universal path that every soul must travel. Kriya Yoga teaches first to withdraw the mind from sensory objects by self control, and then scientifically to disconnect the mind and intelligence from the senses by switching off the life force from the five sense channels, and then take the ego, mind and intellect through the five astral centers in the spine, through the sixth center (the medulla, which is magnetically connected with the spiritual eye in the middle of the forehead), and finally into the seventh center of omniscience in the middle of the cerebrum. The Kriya Yogi then attains perception of his self as soul, and finds his ego, intellect and mind to be dissolved in soul ecstasy. He then learns how to take his soul from the prisons of the physical, astral, and causal bodies and to reunite the soul with Spirit. As the physical eyes through frontal vision, reveal a portion of matter, so the omnipresent spiritual eye, through its boundless spherical visions, reveals the entire astral and ideational cosmoses. In the beginning, when the yogi is able to penetrate his mind through the astral eye, he sees his astral body; by further advancement he sees the entire astral cosmos of which his body is but a part. Without entering the spiritual (astral) eye, no one can know how to take his life force and consciousness through the astral plexuses in the spine. After entering the spiritual eye he passes, in a step by step way, through the perception of the physical body; the perception of the astral eye; the perception of the astral body; the perception of the astral cerebrospinal tunnel with the seven astral plexuses; and through the casual body into final freedom. It requires intricate scientific explanation to interpret Kriya Yoga, but the art itself is very simple. Kriya Yoga, practiced deeply, will dissolve breath into mind, mind into intuition, intuition into the joyous perception of soul, and soul into the cosmic bliss of Spirit. The Yogi then understands how his soul descended into matter and how his prodigal soul has been led from matter back to the mansion of omnipresence, there to enjoy the fatted calf of wisdom".

Detailed instruction in the actual techniques of Kriya Yoga is given to students of the Self Realization Fellowship who fulfill the requirements of certain preliminary spiritual disciplines"...Paramahansa Yogananda wrote: *"In a book available to the general public I cannot give the techniques themselves; for they are sacred, and certain ancient spiritual injections must first be followed to insure that they are received with reverence and confidentiality, and thereafter practiced correctly).*

Appendix 3 – Prayer – Science of Mind – Ernest Holmes

I have covered the subject of meditation from persons far more spiritually advanced and knowledgeable of the subject than myself. Please excuse the copying, but rewording or expressing the information in my own words would most likely distort this very important procedural information about some the techniques for effective meditation. Although I have copied several paragraphs of material, it is only a very small fraction of the material and information provided by these sources. Hopefully the information I provide will lead you to inquire more from those spiritual organizations and literature.

Effective prayer is equally important so I will follow the same process. I provided the information on meditation first because in order to have effective prayer one must learn to go into the trancelike state of meditation where the ego mind cannot interfere. Purification methods are discussed in the next chapter, but perhaps it would be best to cover that information before I provide the reader information on prayer because the purification process leads one into knowing what and what not to pray for. At this point, I would recommend to the reader to begin by praying to Good for Good.

One of the better books on prayer that I have encountered is THE SCIENCE OF MIND by Ernest Holmes: *"The Science of Mind is based entirely upon the supposition that we are surrounded by Good, into which we think. This Good, in Its original state, fills all space. It fills the space that man uses in the Universe. It is in man, as well as outside man. As one thinks into Good, one sets a law in motion, which is creative, and which contains within Itself a limitless possibility. The Good through which man operates is infinite, but man appears to be finite; that is, man has not yet evolved to a complete understanding of himself. The human is unfolding from a limitless potential but can bring into one's experience only that which one can conceive. There is no limit to the Good, but there appears to be a limit to man's understanding of It. As man's understanding unfolds, one's possibilities of attainment will increase."... "Prayer does something to the mind of the one praying. It does not do anything to Good. The eternal gift is always made. The gift of Good is the nature of Good, the eternal giving-ness. Good cannot help making the gift, because Good is the Gift."... "There can be no gift without the receiver. It is said "To as many as received Good, to them Good gave the power. We seek to uncover the science of prayer: the essence of the Good embodied in it. We find that the essence of the power of prayer is faith and acceptance. In addition to the law of faith and acceptance, the law of mental equivalents must be considered. These are the great laws with which we have to deal and we shall never get away from either. If prayer has been answered, it is not because Good has been moved to answer one person and not another, but because one person has moved theirself into a right relationship with Good."... "Since we are thinking beings and cannot stop thinking" (except through meditation) "and since Good receives our thought and cannot stop creating, It must always be creating something for us. What Good will make depends wholly upon what we are thinking, and what we shall attract will depend upon that which our thoughts dwell. Thought can attract to us that which we first mentally embody, that which has become a part of our mental makeup, a part of our inner understanding. Every person is surrounded by a thought atmosphere. This mental atmosphere is the direct result of conscious and unconscious thought, which in it turn, becomes the direct reason for, and cause of that which comes into one's life. Through this power we are either attractive or repelling. Like attracts like and it is also true that we may become attracted to something which is greater than our previous experience."... "One must bring theirself to a place in mind where there is no misfortune, no calamity, no accident, no trouble, no confusion; where there is nothing but plenty, peace, power and Truth. One should definitely, daily (using their own name) declare the Good about theirself, realizing that they are reflecting their statements into consciousness and that they will be operated upon by It. This is called, in mysticism, Good invocation: invoking the Good, implanting within It, seed of thought relative to oneself. And this is why some of the teachers of olden times used to instruct their pupils to cross their hands over their chests and say:" Wonderful, wonderful, wonderful, me!" definitely teaching them that as they mentally held themselves, so they would be held. 'Act as though I am and I will be.' One of the ancient sayings is that "To the person who can perfectly practice inaction, all things are possible." This sounds like a contradiction until one penetrates its inner meaning, for it is only when one completely practices inaction that they arrive at the point of the true actor, for they then realized that the act and the actor are one and the same: that cause and effect are the same: which is simply a different way of saying "Know the truth and the truth shall make you free."*

"*Nothing could bring greater discouragement than to labor under the delusion that an anthropomorphic Good, is a being of moods, who might answer some prayers and not others. It would be difficult to believe in Good who cares more for one person than another. There can be no Good who is kindly disposed one day and cruel the next; there can be no Good who creates us ...and then eternally punishes us when we make a mistake. Good is a universal presence, and impersonal observer, a divine and impartial giver, forever pouring Itsself into Its creation. Most people who believe in Good believe in prayer, but our idea of prayer changes as our idea of Good changes; and it is natural for each to feel that their way of praying is the correct way. But we should bear in mind that the prayers which are effective--no matter whose prayers they may be-- are effective because they embody certain universal principles which, when understood, can be consciously used. If Good ever answered prayer, Good always answers prayer since Good is 'the same yesterday, today and forever'. If there seems to be any failure it is in man's ignorance or misunderstanding of the Will and Nature of Good. We are told that "Good is spirit, and they that worship Good must worship Good in spirit and truth." The immediate availability of the Good is 'neither in the mountain nor at the temple; neither lo, here, nor lo there, for behold the kingdom of Good is within'. This is a true perception of spiritual power. The power is no longer I, but "the Good that dwelleth within me". Could we conceive of Good as being incarnate in us--while at the same time being ever more than that which is incarnated--would we not expand spiritually and intellectually? Would not our prayers be answered before they were uttered? 'The kingdom of Good is within you.' When we become conscious of our oneness with universal Good, beliefs in evil, sin, sickness, limitation, and death tend to disappear. We shall no longer "ask amiss," supplicating as though Good were not willing, begging as though Good were withholding. 'If ye abide in Good and Good abides in you, ye shall ask what ye will and it shall be done unto you.' This gives great light on an important law governing the answering of prayer. Abiding in Good means having no consciousness separate from*

Good consciousness--nothing in our thought which denies the power and presence of Good. Yes, we can readily see why prayers are answered when we are abiding in Good. Again we read, 'Whatsoever ye shall ask in the name of Good, that will Good do'. This sounds simple at first, but it is another profound statement like unto the first; Its significance lies in the phrase: 'in my name'. In Good's name, means like Good's nature. If our thought is as unsullied as the mind of Good, if we are recognizing our oneness with Good, we cannot pray for other than the good of all humans. In such prayer we should not dwell upon evil, sickness or adversity. The secret of spiritual power lies in a consciousness of one's union with the whole, and of the availability of Good. Good is accessible to all people." (SOM)

Naturally, once again, I have edited the above passage to eliminate the many other words used for God, and put the word Good in its place in order for the reader to follow the concept being explained. I also tried to eliminate the masculine gender from the text in order to eliminate that distraction of separating people into genders.

Appendix 4 – Spiritual Treatment

Another method of prayer is called Spiritual Treatment. It is a form of prayer designed to align our mind with our Good. It is taken from a formula that the Lord's Prayer provides: (1) Recognition of our Good, (2) Unification with our Good, (3) Claim, Accept and Express our Good; Deny and eliminate all else. (4) Thanksgiving for our Good. The treatment is in the present tense and we state the facts. First we decide, what is our Good? All words for Good are correct, but remember this method is called Spiritual Treatment and not Material Treatment. Some ideas are happiness, satisfaction, success, contentment, peace, truth, joy. The Recognition statement is: "Our Good is our happiness." The Unification statement is "We are happy". The Claim, Acceptance and Expression statement is "We now claim, accept and express our happiness." The Denial statements ask our Good to remove or dissolve any negative thought forms that would take away our happiness and do not serve our Good. We than thank our Good. The following example is just to show how one can start with prayer treatment:

Title: This treatment is to find and express our Good.

Recognition: Good is
1   Happiness, Satisfaction, Contentment
2   Health, Wealth, Wellbeing
3   Calm Confident, Poised
4   Kind, Loving, Forgiving, Merciful
5   Grateful, Appreciating, Blessed, Praising

Unification: We are
1   Happy, Satisfied and Content
2   Healthy, Wealthy and Well
3   Calm, Confident, Poised
4   Kind, Loving, Forgiving and Merciful

5   Grateful, Appreciating, Blessed, Praising

<u>Claim, Acceptance and Expression</u>: We claim, accept and express
1   Happiness, Satisfaction, Contentment
2   Health, Wealth, Wellbeing
3   Calm, Confidence, Poise
4   Kindness, Love, Forgiveness, Mercy
5   Gratitude, Appreciation, Blessings, Praise

<u>Denial and Elimination</u>: We deny and eliminate
1   Unhappiness, Dissatisfaction, Discontentment
2   Disease, Poverty, Illness
3   Anger, Fear, Worry
4   Cruelty, Hatred, Condemnation, Selfishness
5   Self-centeredness, Ingratitude, Lack, Criticism

<u>Thanksgiving</u>: We give thanks for our
1   Happiness, Satisfaction, Contentment
2   Health, Wealth, Wellbeing
3   Calmness, Confidence, Poise
4   Kindness, Love, Forgiveness, Mercy
5   Gratitude, Appreciation, Blessings, Praise

"Good is _____, We are _____, We claim, accept and express _____, We deny and eliminate _____, We thank you for _____" is perhaps an over-simplification of Spiritual Treatment. The process of speaking or writing more advanced treatments has a tremendous effect on the person praying and the effectiveness of the prayers, but we have to start somewhere. Naturally, the prayer treatment is better conducted using the plural 1st person "We". It has a better effect of joining as one with your brother (friend or foe). The method might be especially useful in praying for your enemies and those you resent. It may help you better see the Holy Spirit in them. From ACIM "Song of Prayer":

Remember our thoughts and beliefs are very powerful and create our experiences. If we experience the same thought over and over again, it becomes a belief or habit. Repeating a treatment can change our habits and beliefs. Choose wisely which new habits and beliefs you want. In order to receive our Good, we must have the belief that we are worthy to receive our Good. We must have the sensation of excitement and empowerment when we are through. In the book <u>Science Of Mind</u> by Ernest Holmes, it states, *"Know, without a shadow of doubt, that as a result of your treatment, some action takes place in Infinite Mind. Infinite Mind is the actor and you are the announcer."* Spiritual treatment is very effective for treating the illness we imagine in the world and replacing it with only Good. The Science Of Mind text tells us that the practitioner *"must be able to look at the sick man who has come to him for help, and know that only perfection stands before him; he must see beyond the appearance to that which is basically perfect."* *"Truth knows no opposites. When we take away the belief in evil, the belief that the outward appearance is the same as the inner reality, evil flees. We must continually remind ourselves of the power of the Word, and of our ability to use it. We must know that Truth produces freedom because Truth is freedom."* Prayer is essential to our Happiness.

Prayer is a very powerful method of helping others. Helping others is altruism and not evangelism. With prayer we don't necessarily have to help others with our mouth, our backs, or our pocket books. The latter is nice but can easily be a trap set up by our Ego for self-praise and adulation. "Hey everybody, look at me and what I have done!" On the other hand, this is not a recommendation to be stingy, selfish, callous and apathetic. We trust the power of our Good and try not to meddle. On this plane of existence, we don't always know when we are being influenced by Spirit or Ego, so therefore we don't know what is best for someone else. In prayer, stick with the basics (e.g. forgiveness, joy, sanity, health, correct thinking, etc.) for yourself and others. Also, in this experience of time, space and matter, it will take some time to develop prayer skills and understanding our inner voice versus our outer emotions. We have work to do along with our Good to get our mind into the condition where we can awaken from the insanity and become aware of what we really are.

The <u>Science Of Mind</u> book points out, *"So we learn to go deeply within ourselves, and speak as though there were a Presence there that knows; and we should take the time to unearth this hidden cause, to penetrate this inner chamber of consciousness. It is most worthwhile to commune with Spirit - to sense and feel It. The approach to Spirit is direct...through our own consciousness. This Spirit flows through us. Whatever intelligence we have is this Spirit in us. Meditation and prayer are their own answer. To daily meditate on the Good, and to daily embody the Great Ideal, is a royal road to freedom, to that peace which passeth understanding, and is happiness to the soul of man. Let us learn to see as Good must, with a Perfect Vision. Let us seek the Good and the True and believe in them with our whole heart, even though everyone we meet seems to be filled with suffering and limitation. We cannot afford to believe in imperfection for to do so is to doubt our Good; it is to believe in a Power apart from our Good and give credence to evil. Let us daily say to ourselves: "Perfect Good within me, Perfect Life within me, come forth into expression through me as that which I am; lead me ever into the paths of Good and cause me to only see, hear, feel, think and act Good."*

Appendix 5 - Spiritual Treatment Meditation

The following is an example guided meditation using a spiritual treatment:

We now ask everyone to take a few seconds to find themselves a comfortable position. We ask that you close your eyes and let the muscles and nerves in your eyelids relax. Think about relaxation and let it happen in your mind. With part of your mind you know that you can always open your eyes, but instead use your imagination to picture your eyes shut. Let the muscles and nerves around and behind your eyes relax. You will not need your vision for the next few minutes, so let your eyes relax. Allow all the muscles and nerves in your face to relax. You will not need your sense of smell or taste so let those nerves going into the brain just relax. Think about your ears and let all the muscles and nerves relax. Just think relaxation and let it happen. Let your temples and forehead relax. Think about your scalp and the base of your skull and let all the muscles and nerves relax.

Now think about your feet and legs and let them relax. It may be a heavy feeling or it may just be a twitch or buzzing feeling, but let your feet and legs relax. Let your buttocks, groin, hips and waist relax. Let your lower and upper abdomen relax. Let your stomach and all your digestive organs relax. Let your breathing and pulse relax. Let all the muscles in your spine, rib cage and back relax. Let all the muscles and nerves in your chest, collar bones, shoulder-blades and under your arms relax. Relax your arms, hands and fingers. Relax your throat and under your chin. Think relaxation.

As I count to three, let your mind picture each letter of the word RELAX and double your relaxation with each letter. You can picture a TV or movie screen or whatever works best for you. One, two, three, see the letter R and double your relaxation. Let the letter R drift away and see the letter E and feel two times more relaxed than just a moment ago. Do this with your mind because you want to feel relaxed and refreshed. Now see the letter L and as the letter L drifts away drop down two more levels of relaxation. Feel a deeper relaxation than you ever felt before. Now let the letter L go and see the letter A and double your relaxation once again; feeling good, whole, refreshed and happy. Let a relaxing smile go upon your face as you let the letter A drift off and see the letter X. Allow yourself with your mind to drift down two more degrees of relaxation.

Now put all your mental, memory and emotional activity on hold for a short while; relax your mind and your subconscious mind and communicate with your Good for a few moments of quiet. Ask it to assist you in denying and removing the negative aspects from your thought, emotions and behavior and actions and lead you into the Good. Pray for sanity in all your endeavors and for knowledge and power to affirm your Good and deny what is no longer your Good. Now, listen and repeat in your mind the following spiritual treatment:

I. Recognition

Denials

- My Good is not hate, sin, evil nor death.
- My Good is not absent, limited nor human.
- My Good is not material, matter nor money.
- My Good is not greed, gluttony, envy nor selfishness.
- My Good is not anger, rage nor violence.
- My Good is not ignorant, vulnerable, controlled nor manipulated.
- My Good is not biased, discriminatory nor prejudice.
- My Good is not turbulence, chaos nor bondage.
- My Good is not defenseless, weak nor frail.
- My Good is not failure, lament, guilt nor shame.
- My Good is not afraid, apprehensive, anxious nor timid.

- My Good is not dreadful, fearsome nor frightful.
- My Good is not imperfect nor impure.
- My Good is not subtractive nor divisive.
- My Good is neither meek nor proud.

Pause

<u>Affirmations</u>

- My Good is love, kindness, forgiveness and mercy.
- My Good is health and sanity in body, mind, emotions and soul.
- My Good is skill, manageability, success, achievement and confidence.
- My Good is joy, happiness, contentment and satisfaction.
- My Good is intelligence, knowledge and wisdom.
- My Good is power, courage, strength and discipline.
- My Good is security, safety, protection and care.
- My Good is imagination, faith, inspiration and enthusiasm.
- My Good is gratitude and appreciation.
- My Good is life, truth and substance.
- My Good is whole and complete.
- My Good is all knowing, ever present and the source of all power.
- My Good is harmony, coherence, amplification and radiance.
- My Good is persistence and perseverance.
- My Good is my voice, word, praise and communication.
- My Good is my sight, hearing, taste, smell, feeling and thinking.
- My Good is balance, equality and equanimity.
- My Good is spiritual, holy and moral.
- My Good is perfect, noble and glorious.
- My Good is vitality, vigor and consistency.
- My Good is dedication, conviction and miraculous.
- My Good is additive, multiplying and exponential.

- My Good is growing, expanding and all encompassing.
- My Good is perfect demonstration, perfect character, perfect healing, perfect composure, divine joy and blessed happiness.

Pause

II. Unification

Denials (Singular, 1st person)

- In Good, I am not hate, sin, evil nor death.
- In Good, I am not absent, limited nor human.
- In Good, I am not material, matter nor money.
- In Good, I am not greed, gluttony, envy nor selfishness.
- In Good, I am not anger, rage nor violence.
- In Good, I am is not ignorant, vulnerable, controlled nor manipulated.
- In Good, I am not biased, discriminatory nor prejudice.
- In Good, I am not turbulence, chaos nor bondage.
- In Good, I am not defenseless, weak nor frail.
- In Good, I am not failure, lament, guilt nor shame.
- In Good, I am not afraid, apprehensive, anxious nor timid.
- In Good, I am not dreadful, fearsome nor frightful.
- In Good, I am not imperfect nor impure.
- In Good, I am not subtractive nor divisive.
- In Good, I am neither meek nor proud.

Pause

Affirmations (Singular, 1st person)

- In Good, I am love, kindness, forgiveness and mercy.
- In Good, I am health and sanity in body, mind, emotions and soul.

- In Good, I am skill, manageability, success, achievement and confidence.
- In Good, I am joy, happiness, contentment and satisfaction.
- In Good, I am intelligence, knowledge and wisdom.
- In Good, I am power, courage, strength and discipline.
- In Good, I am security, safety, protection and care.
- In Good, I am imagination, faith, inspiration and enthusiasm.
- In Good, I am gratitude and appreciation.
- In Good, I am life, truth and substance.
- In good, I am whole and complete.
- In Good, I am all knowing, ever present and the source of all power.
- In Good, I am harmony, coherence, amplification and radiance.
- In Good, I am persistence and perseverance.
- In Good, I am voice, word, praise and communication.
- In Good, I am healthy sight, hearing, taste, smell, feeling and thinking.
- In Good, I am balance, equality and equanimity.
- In Good, I am spiritual, holy and moral.
- In Good, I am perfect, noble and glorious.
- In Good, I am vitality, vigor and consistency.
- In Good, I am dedication, conviction and miraculous.
- In Good, I am additive, multiplying and exponential.
- In Good, I am growing, expanding and all encompassing.
- In Good, I am perfect demonstration, perfect character, perfect healing, perfect composure, divine joy and blessed happiness.

Pause

Denials (2nd person)

- In Good, you are not hate, sin, evil nor death.
- In Good, you are not absent, limited nor human.

- In Good, you are not material, matter nor money.
- In Good, you are not greed, gluttony, envy nor selfishness.
- In Good, you are not anger, rage nor violence.
- In Good, you are not ignorant, vulnerable, controlled nor manipulated.
- In Good, you are not biased, discriminatory nor prejudice.
- In Good, you are not turbulence, chaos nor bondage.
- In Good, you are not defenseless, weak nor frail.
- In Good, you are not failure, lament, guilt nor shame.
- In Good, you are not afraid, apprehensive, anxious nor timid.
- In Good, you are not dreadful, fearsome nor frightful.
- In Good, you are not imperfect nor impure.
- In Good, you are not subtractive nor divisive.
- In Good, you are neither meek nor proud.

Pause

Affirmations (2nd person)

- In Good, you are love, kindness, forgiveness and mercy.
- In Good, you are health and sanity in body, mind, emotions and soul.
- In Good, you are skill, manageability, success, achievement and confidence.
- In Good, you are joy, happiness, contentment and satisfaction.
- In Good, you are intelligence, knowledge and wisdom.
- In Good, you are power, courage, strength and discipline.
- In Good, you are security, safety, protection and care.
- In Good, you are imagination, faith, inspiration and enthusiasm.
- In Good, you are gratitude and appreciation.
- In Good, you are life, truth and substance.
- In Good, you are whole and complete.

- In Good, you are all knowing, ever present and the source of all power.
- In Good, you are harmony, coherence, amplification and radiance.
- In Good, you are persistence and perseverance.
- In Good, you are voice, word, praise and communication.
- In Good, you are healthy sight, hearing, taste, smell, feeling and thinking.
- In Good, you are balance, equality and equanimity.
- In Good, you are spiritual, holy and moral.
- In Good, you are perfect, noble and glorious.
- In Good, you are vitality, vigor and consistency.
- In Good, you are dedication, conviction and miraculous.
- In Good, you are additive, multiplying and exponential.
- In Good, you are growing, expanding and all encompassing.
- In Good, you are perfect demonstration, perfect character, perfect healing, perfect composure, divine joy and blessed happiness.

Pause

Denials (3rd person)

- In Good, he and she (they) are not hate, sin, evil or death.
- In Good, he and she (they) are not absent, limited or human.
- In Good, he and she (they) are not material, matter nor money.
- In Good, he and she (they) are not greed, gluttony, envy or selfishness.
- In Good, he and she (they) are not anger, rage or violence.
- In Good, he and she (they) are not ignorant, vulnerable, controlled or manipulated.
- In Good, he and she (they) are not biased, discriminatory or prejudice.

- In Good, he and she (they) are not turbulence, chaos or bondage.
- In Good, he and she (they) are not defenseless, weak and frail.
- In Good, he and she (they) are not failure, lament, guilt and shame.
- In Good, he and she (they) are not afraid, apprehensive, anxious or timid.
- In Good, he and she (they) are not dreadful, fearsome or frightful.
- In Good, he and she (they) are not imperfect or impure.
- In Good, he and she (they) are not subtractive or divisive.
- In Good, he and she (they) are neither meek nor proud.

Pause

Affirmations (3rd person)

- In Good, he and she (they) are love, kindness, forgiveness and mercy.
- In Good, he and she (they) are health and sanity in body, mind, emotions and soul.
- In Good, he and she (they) are skill, manageability, success, achievement and confidence.
- In Good, he and she (they) are joy, happiness, contentment and satisfaction.
- In Good, he and she (they) are intelligence, knowledge and wisdom.
- In Good, he and she (they) are power, courage, strength and discipline.
- In Good, he and she (they) are security, safety, protection and care.
- In Good, he and she (they) are imagination, faith, inspiration and enthusiasm.
- In Good, he and she (they) are gratitude and appreciation.
- In Good, he and she (they) are life, truth and substance.

- In Good, he and she (they) are whole and complete.
- In Good, he and she (they) are all knowing, ever present and the source of all power.
- In Good, he and she (they) are harmony, coherence, amplification and radiance.
- In Good, he and she (they) are persistence and perseverance.
- In Good, he and she (they) are voice, word, praise and communication.
- In Good, he and she (they) are healthy sight, hearing, taste, smell, feeling and thinking.
- In Good, he and she (they) are balance, equality and equanimity.
- In Good, he and she (they) are spiritual, holy and moral.
- In Good, he and she (they) are perfect, noble and glorious.
- In Good, he and she (they) are vitality, vigor and consistency.
- In Good, he and she (they) are dedication, conviction and miraculous.
- In Good, he and she (they) are additive, multiplying and exponential.
- In Good, he and she (they) are growing, expanding and all encompassing.
- In Good, he and she (they) are perfect demonstration, perfect character, perfect healing, perfect composure, divine joy and blessed happiness.

Pause

Denials (Plural, 1st person)

- In Good, we are not hate, sin, evil or death.
- In Good, we are not absent, limited or human.
- In Good, we are not material, matter nor money.
- In Good, we are not greed, gluttony, envy or selfishness.
- In Good, we are not anger, rage or violence.

- In Good, we are is not ignorant, vulnerable, controlled or manipulated.
- In Good, we are not biased, discriminatory or prejudice.
- In Good, we are not turbulence, chaos or bondage.
- In Good, we are not defenseless, weak and frail.
- In Good, we are not failure, lament, guilt and shame.
- In Good, we are not afraid, apprehensive, anxious or timid.
- In Good, we are not dreadful, fearsome or frightful.
- In Good, we are not imperfect or impure.
- In Good, we are not subtractive or divisive.
- In Good, we are neither meek nor proud.

Pause

<u>Affirmations</u> (Plural, 1st person)

- In Good, we are love, kindness, forgiveness and mercy.
- In Good, we are health and sanity in body, mind, emotions and soul.
- In Good, we are skill, manageability, success, achievement and confidence.
- In Good, we are joy, happiness, contentment and satisfaction.
- In Good, we are intelligence, knowledge and wisdom.
- In Good, we are power, courage, strength and discipline.
- In Good, we are security, safety, protection and care.
- In Good, we are imagination, faith, inspiration and enthusiasm.
- In Good, we are gratitude and appreciation.
- In Good, we are life, truth and substance.
- In Good, we are whole and complete.
- In Good, we are all knowing, ever present and the source of all power.
- In Good, we are harmony, coherence, amplification and radiance.
- In Good, we are persistence and perseverance.

- In Good, we are voice, word, praise and communication.
- In Good, we are healthy sight, hearing, taste, smell, feeling and thinking.
- In Good, we are balance, equality and equanimity.
- In Good, we are spiritual, holy and moral.
- In Good, we are perfect, noble and glorious.
- In Good, we are vitality, vigor and consistency.
- In Good, we are dedication, conviction and miraculous.
- In Good, we are additive, multiplying and exponential.
- In Good, we are growing, expanding and all encompassing.
- In Good, we are perfect demonstration, perfect character, perfect healing, perfect composure, divine joy and blessed happiness.

Pause

III. Declaration

We now uncover, declare, claim, manifest, accept, exhibit, express and demonstrate:

- love, kindness, forgiveness and mercy.
- health and sanity, body, mind, emotions and soul.
- skill, manageability, success, achievement and confidence.
- joy, happiness, contentment and satisfaction.
- intelligence, knowledge and wisdom.
- power, courage, strength and discipline.
- security, safety, protection and care.
- imagination, faith, inspiration and enthusiasm.
- gratitude and appreciation.
- life, truth and substance.
- wholeness and completion.
- all knowing, ever present and the source of all power.
- harmony, coherence, amplification and radiance.
- persistence and perseverance.
- voice, words, praise and communication.

- healthy sight, hearing, taste, smell, feeling and thinking.
- balance, equality and equanimity.
- spiritual, holy and moral.
- perfection, morality, nobility and glory.
- vitality, vigor and consistency.
- dedication, conviction and miracles.
- additive, multiplying and exponential Good.
- growing, expanding and all encompassing Good.
- perfect demonstration, perfect character, perfect healing, perfect composure, divine joy and blessed happiness.

Pause

IV. Thanksgiving:

I eat from the banquet of Good Life and enjoy the many different delicious tastes provided me. I do not settle for a grain of rice, but dine and enjoy to my fullest. I give thanks for all the Good that is expressed before me now and so It is.

Pause

Now as I count from one to five, I ask you to come back to your normal awakened state at a higher level of consciousness of your Good happening here and now. One: feel yourself being lifted up and out of what is no longer your Good. Two: Feel the presence of a loving, benevolent, powerful and intelligent Good joining forces with you. Three: See yourself within your desired Good. Four: Feel yourself smiling, being happy, joyous and free. Five: Come back to a spiritually and morally awake state of mind, completely aware of your Good in the here and now, superior to anything you have ever experienced in this life.

Pause

Now to make sure that we are fully conscious and awake to

prevent anyone from leaving and returning home in a trance, please state together out loud, "We are now awake and alert to our surroundings."

Made in the USA
Las Vegas, NV
22 December 2021